HENRY TRUCKS

PAINTER

HENRYTRUCKS

PAINTER

ancient myths meet modern landscapes | 1995–2010

SACRAMENTO, CALIFORNIA

THE ARCHITECT PAINTER PRESS

JEF7REY HILDNER

BOOKS BY JEF7REY HILDNER (aka ELIOT PLUM and HENRY TRUCKS) :

AUTHOR, BOOK DESIGNER, AND PUBLISHER
LIVE BRAVE: A Tribute To Laura Middleton
VISUAL EF9ECTS | Architecture and the Chess Game of Form & Story
METAPHYSICAL WARRIOR: Meditations on the art & science of life
DAEDALUS 9 | THE ARCHITECT PAINTER [improv 1.0]
HENRY TRUCKS — Painter : ancient myths meet modern landscapes | 1995–2010
MISFITZ BECAUSE: What Doesn't Belong—and Why? Mind-Teasers!
GARCHES 1234 | Remembering the Mathematics of the Ideal Villa: An Essay on Le Corbusier's 1927 Villa de Monzie/Stein
PICASSO LESSONS: The Sixth Woman of Les Demoiselles d'Avignon

CONTRIBUTOR
ARCHITECTURAL FORMALISM, by Hakan Anay—with Rosalind Krauss, Peggy Deamer, Robert Slutzky, and Colin Rowe
REMEMBRANCE AND THE DESIGN OF PLACE, by Frances Downing
CONNECTIVE TISSUES: Ten Essays by University of Virginia Kenan Fellows 2001–2016, by Peter Waldman | Epilogue: "Labyrinth R.U.N."

HENRY TRUCKS — PAINTER : ancient myths meet modern landscapes | 1995–2010

THANK YOU: Richard Rosa—artistic ally who invited me to participate in the Symposium on Formalism at the Syracuse University School of Architecture Program in Florence. Preparing my talk for that February 2016 symposium inspired me to write the book *VISUAL EF9ECTS—Architecture and the Chess Game of Form & Story*, which led me to revise the titles of some of my paintings in this edition, more clearly conveying the chess-based themes that have shaped my work for years; George Gintole—visual mentor who set me on the path of architecture as art; David Zlowe—brave patron and owner of Dante | Telescope House, which so far most fully expresses the ideals of The Architect Painter; Richard "Smoke" Atchison—skillful fabricator of the frames for *Ulysses* and *Daedalus* from aluminum we found at a stockyard in Fort Worth, Texas; Generous patrons and benefactors—Ellen Peckham of AE Ventures Foundation, Alex & Patrick Magness, Michele & Chip Chandler, Sho-Ping Chin & David Chan, Kelly & Mark Hildner, and John Lanasa & Paul Davis. And with all my heart, thank you, my beautiful copyeditor and patron, role model of courage, equanimity, and grace, my hero, advisor, cheerleader, and loyal, steadfast friend of 35 years, and my partner for the last 3½ years of her life: Laura Dawn Middleton. November 27, 1963 – November 29, 2017. Where did you go, Laura?

ARCHITECT, PAINTER, AND WRITER JEF7REY HILDNER AKA HENRY TRUCKS launched The Architect Painter Press in 2005 under the banner, "Live Brave." The Architect Painter Press presents Hildner's buildings, paintings, and insights—work that reflects his focus on the visible and invisible architecture of art and life. The Architect Painter Press also seeks to present the work of other artists. Current titles range from Hildner's books *Visual Ef9ects*, *Daedalus 9*, *Henry Trucks — Painter*, *Picasso Lessons*, and *Garches 1234* to his books *Metaphysical Warrior* and *Live Brave*. His work also appears in a wide array of venues beyond the pages of The Architect Painter Press—for example, *Architectural Record*, *ANY*, *Oz*, IMDb, *Journal of Architectural Education*, and *Global Architecture Houses*. The book *Architectural Formalism*, by Hakan Anay, features Hildner's essay "Formalism: Move | Meaning" alongside essays by theorists Rosalind Krauss, Peggy Deamer, Robert Slutzky, and Colin Rowe. The book *Connective Tissues*, by Peter Waldman, features Hildner's Epilogue, "Labyrinth R.U.N." Hildner received an Association of Collegiate Schools of Architecture award for excellence in teaching. His project Dante | Telescope House won the New Jersey Chapter of The American Institute of Architects "Blue Ribbon Award for Excellence in Design." He paints under the name Henry Trucks. He writes under the names Madison Gray, Eliot Plum, and Michelangelo A. Roland Slate. Hildner's one-word life theme—architecture—shapes his quest, his outlook, and his output, including his work as screenwriter and story architect. He earned his undergraduate and graduate degrees from Princeton University.

BOOK WRITTEN, CREATED, DESIGNED, AND PRODUCED BY JEF7REY HILDNER

For my daughter, Emily—Soul visible

"I DRAW NO DISTINCTION BETWEEN THE CONSTRUCTION OF A BOOK AND THE CONSTRUCTION OF A PAINTING." —HENRI MATISSE

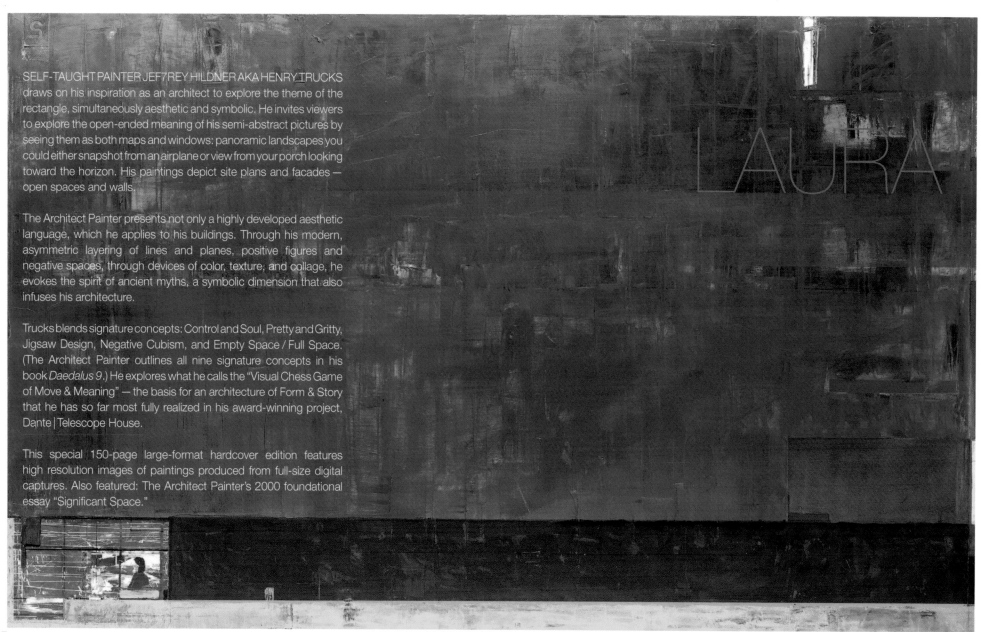

SELF-TAUGHT PAINTER JEF7REY HILDNER AKA HENRY TRUCKS
draws on his inspiration as an architect to explore the theme of the
rectangle, simultaneously aesthetic and symbolic. He invites viewers
to explore the open-ended meaning of his semi-abstract pictures by
seeing them as both maps and windows: panoramic landscapes you
could either snapshot from an airplane or view from your porch looking
toward the horizon. His paintings depict site plans and facades —
open spaces and walls.

The Architect Painter presents not only a highly developed aesthetic
language, which he applies to his buildings. Through his modern,
asymmetric layering of lines and planes, positive figures and
negative spaces, through devices of color, texture, and collage, he
evokes the spirit of ancient myths, a symbolic dimension that also
infuses his architecture.

Trucks blends signature concepts: Control and Soul, Pretty and Gritty,
Jigsaw Design, Negative Cubism, and Empty Space / Full Space.
(The Architect Painter outlines all nine signature concepts in his
book *Daedalus 9*.) He explores what he calls the "Visual Chess Game
of Move & Meaning" — the basis for an architecture of Form & Story
that he has so far most fully realized in his award-winning project,
Dante | Telescope House.

This special 150-page large-format hardcover edition features
high resolution images of paintings produced from full-size digital
captures. Also featured: The Architect Painter's 2000 foundational
essay "Significant Space."

Art presents more than meets the eye.

"I rhyme [I paint] . . . to see myself, to set the darkness echoing." —Seamus Heaney

THE SILVER KNIGHT
OF ART

MY AVATAR

**?+_###@|~~~——

SIGNIFICANTSPACE

ART IS A CHESS GAME OF FORM & STORY WAGED ON THE BATTLEFIELD OF OUR MIND AND SOUL AND HEART

THE ARMIES OF FORM & STORY FIGHT THE WAR OF ART
THEY FIGHT FOR OUR MIND AND SOUL AND HEART

THE SILVER KNIGHT OF FORM & STORY

"All art tends towards structuring the contradiction between that which appears and that which signifies, between form and meaning."

—Robert Slutzky, "Re-Reading Phenomenal Transparency"

Through painting, I seek to find the Significant Form & Significant Space of my architecture.

why i paint + significant space + move & meaning

Through painting, I foreshadow an architecture of Form & Story.

"All art tends towards structuring the contradiction between that which appears and that which signifies, between form and meaning."

—Robert Slutzky, "Re-Reading Phenomenal Transparency"

THEORY
why i paint + significant space + move & meaning

Through painting, I seek to find
the Significant Form & Significant Space of my architecture.

why i paint + significant space + **move & meaning**

WHY I PAINT. In the fall of 1995, I began to teach myself to paint. A licensed architect, I was teaching at the University of Virginia, conducting a graduate architecture design studio and a graduate theory seminar on the emergence of abstraction in modern art. Up to that point, I had made works on paper—collages and drawings in gouache and ink—and had created several buildings, most notably *Dante/Telescope House*, for which I had painted murals and designed rugs and sandblasted glass (images below). I was ready to become a painter. I knew why I wanted to paint and the concepts I wanted to explore. So I made the leap. And I'm glad I did. It "has made all the difference." [1]

One of my first paintings: **OBSERVATORY**, 1995. Oil, collage, and pencil (charcoal, graphite) on canvas. 8 x 10 in. Private Collection, New York, NY

F O R M &

WHY I PAINT

[1] "Two roads diverged in a wood, and I— / I took the one less traveled by, / And that has made all the difference." —Robert Frost, "The Road Not Taken"

Painting allows pure artistic freedom.

No client or contractor factors into the equation.

No editor makes changes.

Time and money don't shape the work.

I strive to honor the timeless slogan of the pioneer-artist:

"My work, done my way."

Which doesn't mean that I made these paintings uninfluenced

by artistic forces outside of myself.

Mentor-heroes have equipped me with compass and lantern for my journey.

Painters: Diebenkorn, Mondrian, Matisse, Braque, Picasso, Gris, van Doesburg, Kondos, Thiebaud, Malevich, Nicholson, Avery.

Architects: Le Corbusier, Schindler, Rietveld, Hadid, Olgiati, Waldman, Graves, Hejduk, Eisenman, Barragán, Gaudi, Terragni.

Through painting,

I seek to find the Significant Form & Significant Space of my architecture.

Through painting,

I foreshadow an architecture of Form & Story.

S   T   O   R   Y

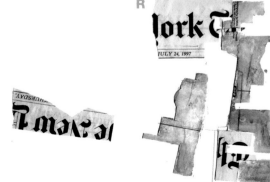

DESIGNING THE VISUAL FIELD | THE ARCHITECTURE OF FORM AND SPACE. My work explores ideas and themes that spring from my research into the theory of art. I highlight one central theme in the following essay (p. 24) that I wrote in 2000: "**SIGNIFICANT SPACE**."

Opposite: My first painting—*SPACECRAFT*, 1995. Acrylic, collage, and pencil (grease, charcoal, graphite) on canvas. 24 x 36 in.

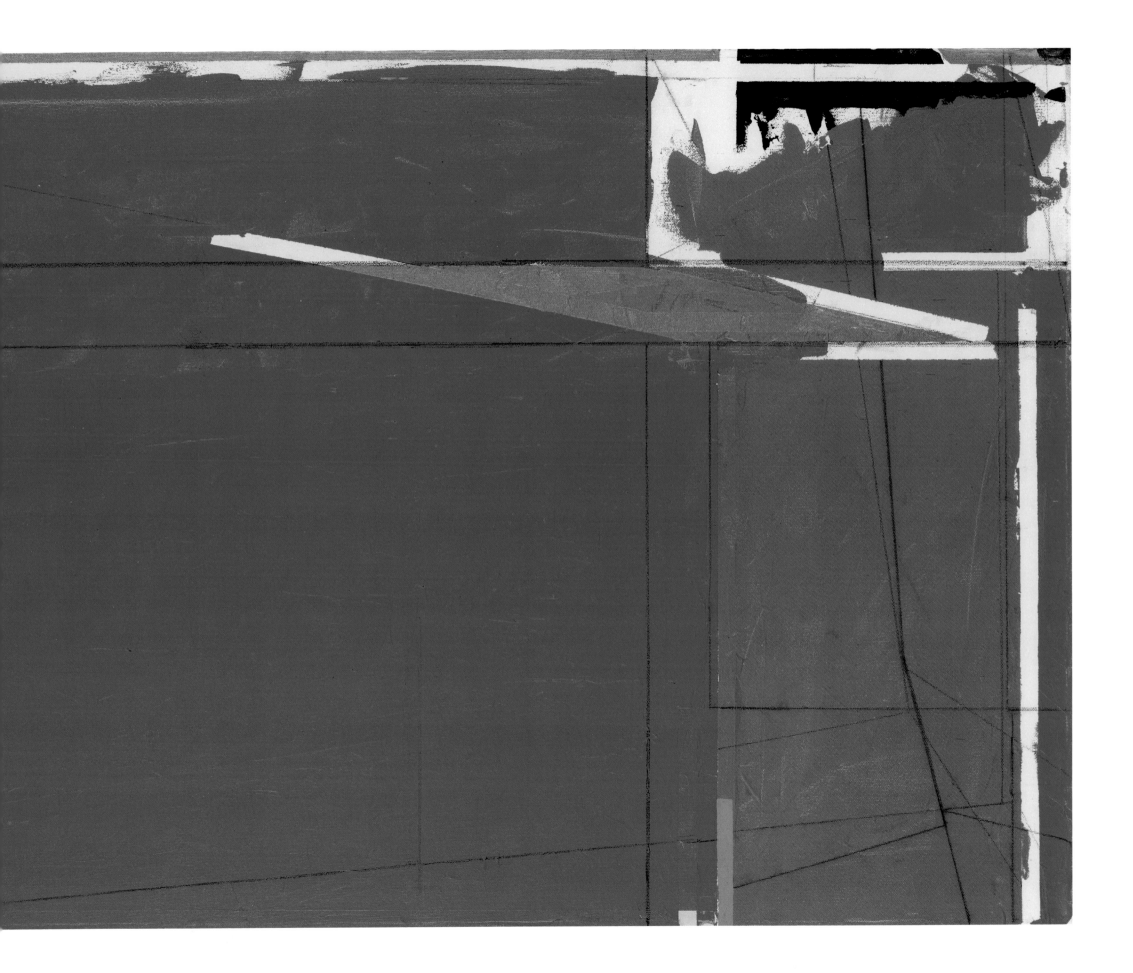

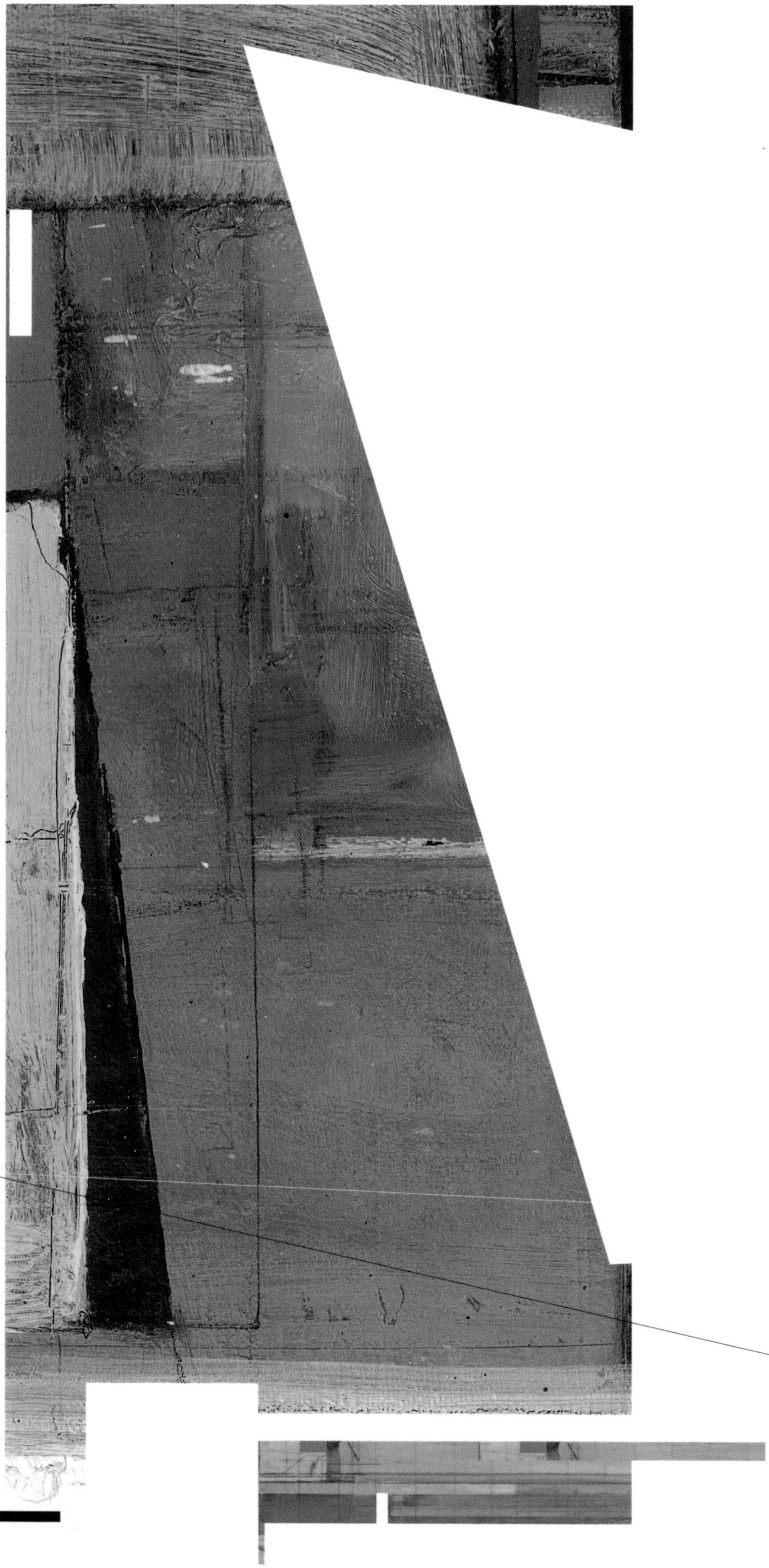

Graylands, 1995. Acrylic and pencil (charcoal, graphite) on canvas. 16 x 20 in.

SIGNIFICANT SPACE

Turning a negative into a positive in the landscapes (and walls) of modern art

24 HENRY TRUCKS

1 *Mont Sainte-Victoire Seen from the Bibemus Quarry*, c. 1897. Paul Cézanne. Oil on canvas. 25.5 x 32 in. The Baltimore Museum of Art. © Public Domain.
2 *Seated Figure with Hat*, 1967. Richard Diebenkorn. Oil on canvas. 60 x 60 in. (152.4 x 152.4 cm). Estate #1412. © The Richard Diebenkorn Foundation.
3 *Ocean Park #54*, 1972. Richard Diebenkorn. Oil and charcoal on canvas. 100 x 81 in. (254 x 205.7 cm). Estate #1469. © The Richard Diebenkorn Foundation.

1   2   3

NEGATIVE AND POSITIVE attributes of matter at the atomic level preoccupied advanced physicists at the start of the 20th century. J.J. Thomson discovered the electron in 1897. Ernest Rutherford named the proton in 1919. During the same time frame, negative/positive issues involving the visual structure of human-scale space and form preoccupied avant-garde painters.

Cézanne, Matisse, Malevich, Picasso, Braque—these and other artists invented what British art critic Clive Bell famously described in his classic 1914 book, *Art*, as "Significant Form." They didn't try to record a camera-accurate view of the exterior world. They created pictures that broke free, in minor and major ways, from ordinary perception. Artists made paintings according to their own rules. Form, these artists asserted, has aesthetic value and meaning—*significance*—in its own right. The true value of form doesn't spring from how well it corresponds with nature or to the way the world looks to those who don't make art.

In addition to research into Significant Form, painters also explored what I term "Significant Space." Space that leaps to the foreground in the hierarchy of the form-space visual field. Space that becomes no less form than form itself. Space that radiates compositional importance and influence as well as, ideally, symbolic meaning. Modern, abstract art in large measure evolved from the interplay of these complementary concepts: SIGNIFICANT FORM & SIGNIFICANT SPACE.

One of the major expressions of Significant Space involves what artists and designers call "negative space." When we look at an object, we see space around the object. We typically regard the object as the positive element and the space around the object as the negative element. Modern painters activated this negative element: They designed the surrounding space that an object generates. They treated space as form! Setting up a yin-yang ambiguity between positive and negative elements in a picture, painters gave spaces figural identity equal in compositional value to objects. In other words, they treated the solids (positive objects) and voids (negative spaces) as interdependent abstract elements of the visual field. In keeping with Mondrian's manifesto, "The modern artist is the conscious artist," modern painters consciously designed the relationships between figural solids and figural voids.

How important was this? Painter Joseph Albers summed it up this way: "Perhaps the only entirely new and probably the most important aspect of today's language of forms is the fact that 'negative' elements (the remainder, intermediate, and subtractive quantities) are made active" ("Creative Education," Sixth International Congress for Drawing, Art Education, and Applied Art, Prague, 1928).

OBJECT/BACKGROUND : FIGURE/GROUND : "FIGURE|FIELD." For the fountainhead of this idea, which also influenced modern photography, sculpture, and architecture, we look to Cézanne. His painting *Mont Sainte-Victoire Seen from the Bibemus Quarry* (illustration 1), for example, depicts (as the painting's title tells us) a mountain and a quarry. But Cézanne also gave a major role to the sky. He made it the largest shape in the composition and treated it as Significant Space: compositionally important negative space. Through size, shape, and contour, Cézanne gave the sky as much visual weight as the mountain with which it figurally interlocks. And Cézanne crafted their mutual outline with self-conscious élan: He juxtaposed the resolute razor-sharp edge of the left side to the meandering jagged edge of the right. The sky conventionally defines the background against which we see an object such as a mountain—the "ground" or "field" (my term) against which we see a "figure." But Cézanne didn't treat the sky as a background or leftover space. He treated the sky as a carefully designed figure. He created what art critic Patrick Heron calls "solid space" (see his essay "Solid space in Cézanne," *Modern Painters*, Spring 1996, pp. 16–24). And through the device of object/background ambiguity—typically called "figure/ground" ambiguity (or what I term "Figure|Field" ambiguity)— Cézanne turned mountain and sky into a basic art lesson. Quirky, interdependent shapes arranged on a flat surface, warm mountain and cool sky oscillate between their roles as solid and void and demonstrate textbook equilibrium between positive object and negative space.

Likewise, Cézanne upends our perception of the spatial position of mountain and sky. Actually just paint, they function as pieces of a jigsaw puzzle—neither piece in front of the other. By treating the elements of his abstract design this way, Cézanne causes the space between sky, mountain, quarry, and foreground trees to fluctuate. This into-the-picture space, which I term "atmospheric space," appears shallow one moment, deep the next (see "Deep Space/Shallow Space," by Thomas Schumacher, *Architectural Review*, January 1987, pp. 37–42). Our perception of deep space reinforces the illusion of perspective while our perception of shallow space reinforces the truth of the painting's flat surface.

Cézanne-like negative space, as filtered principally through the works of Mondrian and Matisse, became a central concern of Richard Diebenkorn 70 years later in his painting *Seated Figure with Hat* (illustration 2). Diebenkorn didn't regard the background as an afterthought. He made the background as figural as the seated "Figure" of the painting's title. And in a crucial move more modern than Cézanne, Diebenkorn even shifted the woman to one side, decentering her and giving the background's negative space center stage. The shared undulating contour of the background and the woman, running diagonally from her knee, along her lap, and up over her hat—an echo of the contour of the right side of Mont Sainte-Victoire—creates a beautiful, poignant event. In various ways, Diebenkorn clearly signals that within the painting's square field of visual activity, the woman has no more artistic significance than the scumbled-yellow abstract space-forms that embrace her and give her shape.

Which raises a related issue: Does the yellow negative space comprise a wall against which the woman is sitting? Or is she sitting in the foreground of a sun-drenched landscape that extends to the horizon line at the top of the painting? In the first case, we see the space—the atmospheric space—between the woman and the yellow wall as compressed, closed, vertically bounded by the x/y plane. In a word: shallow. In the second, we regard the atmospheric space beyond the woman as receding along the ground plane to the horizon line. Space strikes us as extended, open, horizontally expansive along the z-axis. In a word: deep. This ambiguity between shallow and deep space underscores the tension, as in the Cézanne, between the truth of the two-dimensionality of the canvas—a painted flat surface—and the illusion of three-dimensional depth. And Diebenkorn amps up the 2D/3D tension with the emotional charge of California sunshine. The result: More than visibly interlocked, the woman and the landscape become also invisibly interlocked. Diebenkorn blends the cool contemplative peace of the woman's inner world with the warm robust promise of her outer world. And this interdependence between the visible design elements and the emotional, psychological elements creates Significant Space that radiates both compositional value *and* symbolic meaning.

In the brilliant Ocean Park series that he began the next year, and continued to pursue into the 1980s, Diebenkorn removed the anthropomorphic figure. As in this representative painting, *Ocean Park No. 54* (illustration 3), he treated space and space-forms as the active essence of his art. He crafted an abstract, rectilinear architecture of ambiguity and equilibrium between complementary elements: positive and negative, solid and void, figure and field, orthogonal structure and diagonal inflection—between flat surface and infinite depth. Like many of his Bay Area Figurative paintings, such as *Seated Figure with Hat,* Diebenkorn's radical Ocean Park paintings distill the lessons of Cézanne's French mountains and skies and extend and transpose these lessons to the luminous Pacific beachfront of Southern California: the land "out West" that promises unlimited horizons.

Diebenkorn's Ocean Park paintings—which I call semiabstract "Figure|Field" paintings—represent walls and windows (i.e., vertical surfaces/facades—composed of transparent, translucent, and opaque materials), as well as landscapes (i.e., aerial maps/site plans). I see these walls and landscapes as light-reflective, electromagnetic aesthetic fields that are at the same time highly charged and neutral. And I think Diebenkorn's works, including his earlier, figural space-making pictures, resonate with instruction for advanced painters and architects today.

SPACECRAFT. I build on what I see in Diebenkorn's paintings in my work. I build also on what I see in the work of other space-maker painters, sculptors, photographers, and architects.[1] Throughout this book—through page layouts, book covers, collages, drawings, graphic studies, paintings, and buildings—I show various ways that I try to *spacecraft* Significant Space and create a language of space-defining form and form-defining space.

[1] For example: Georges Braque (*Still life with a violin*, 1912), Pablo Picasso (*The Violin*, 1912), Milton Avery (*Nude In Black Robe*, 1950); Sam Francis (Untitled [Edge Painting], 1966); Henry Moore (*Seated Figure Against Curved Wall*, 1956–57); Arnold Newman ("Portrait of Edward Hopper," 1941); Rudolph Schindler (Kings Road House, 1922). See these examples in the online version of this essay: https://archive.org/details/SignificantSpace.

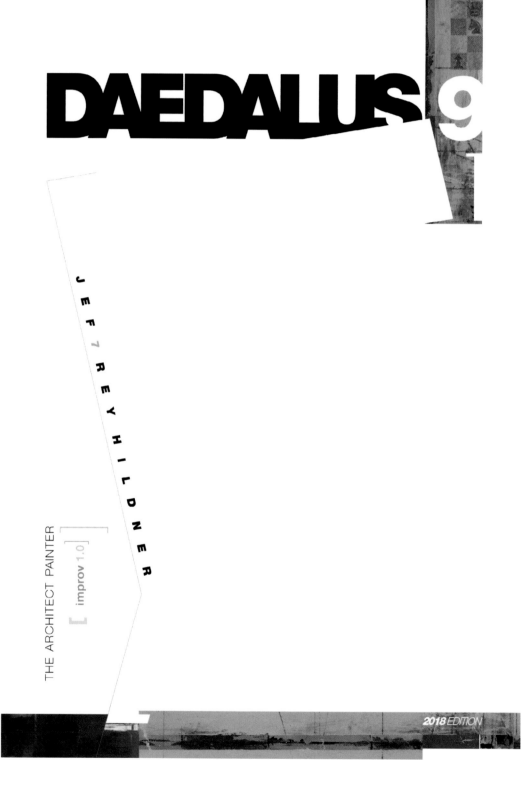

SPACE-DEFINING FRAGMENTS. *JIGSAW No. 1 | NYT*, 2013. Digital collage on canvas: collage on paper + oil on canvas. 14 x 26 in. Note the "p" for positive and "n" for negative that label a major space-making device that I term **Knight's Move**, one of the many devices that create a matrix of Significant Space, including another trademark device that I term **Jigsaw Design**.

ARCHITECTURE ORIENTS US IN THE WORLD
— and inspires us to look deep into the nature of reality.

The steel-beam telescope (a shard of ancient suns) sights the North Star . . .

A WALL IS A CANVAS. AND A CANVAS IS A WALL.
A SITE PLAN IS A CANVAS. AND A CANVAS IS A SITE PLAN.

SIGNIFICANT SPACE

SIGNIFICANT SPACE: Central Park, Manhattan, 1995. Gouache and pencil (charcoal, graphite) on paper. 18 x 24 in.

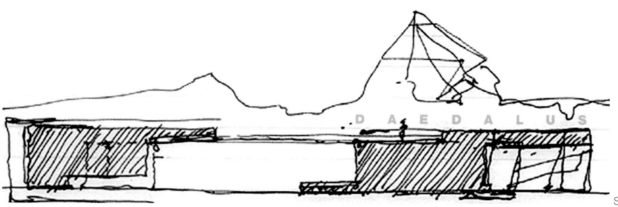

SKETCH FOR **THE DAEDALUS PROJECT: THE HERO'S JOURNEY HOUSE**

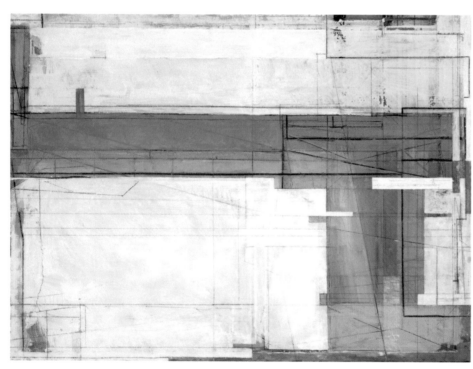

DAEDALUS'S LABYRINTH, 1997. Oil and pencil (grease, charcoal, graphite) on canvas. 18 x 24 in.

CRETE, 1998. Oil and pencil (graphite) on canvas. 36 x 60 in.

PAINT SPACE | REAL SPACE. Some Significant Space asserts importance compositionally but not symbolically—for example, the sky in Cézanne's *Mont Sainte-Victoire Seen from the Bibemus Quarry* (p. 25). On the other hand, some Significant Space asserts importance symbolically but not compositionally—for example, someone's study in a tract house. But when fully realized, Significant Space strikes a beautiful balance between the two types of significance and resonates with both compositional and symbolical importance, as we see and feel in the Paint Space of Diebenkorn's pictures, such as *Seated Figure with Hat* and *Ocean Park No. 54* (p. 25), and in the Real Space of Olmsted & Vaux's Central Park and Jefferson's UVA Lawn.

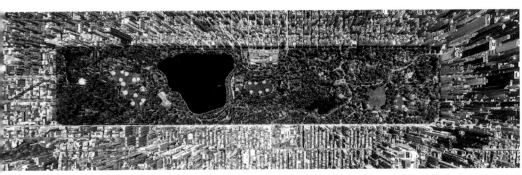

CENTRAL PARK, NYC. FREDERICK LAW OLMSTED & CALVERT VAUX, 1857–1873

THE LAWN. THOMAS JEFFERSON, 1817.

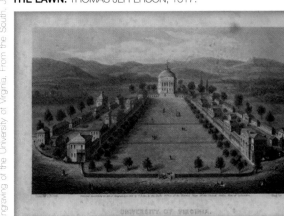

LABYRINTH ii, 1998. Oil and pencil (grease, charcoal, graphite) on canvas. 30 x 40 in. Private Collection, Boston, MA

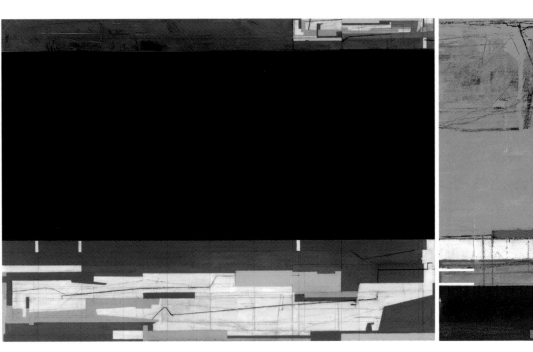

TEMPLE OF THE ANCIENT KNIGHT, 1997. Acrylic and pencil (grease, charcoal, graphite) on canvas. 30 x 40 in.

EMPTY SPACE | FULL SPACE. I explore through my paintings the theme of the rectangle, including what I call the Empty Rectangle—expressed primarily as an Empty Center defined by a Full Edge. Iconic examples: Manhattan's Central Park by Olmsted & Vaux and the University of Virginia's Academical Village, organized around The Lawn, Thomas Jefferson's sublime open space, physically empty but metaphysically full.

FIGURE | FIELD

SIGNIFICANT SPACE

You can fill space with the elements of form, or you can shape space with the elements of form. You can design forms that occupy space, or you can design forms that define space — you can design the solid and the void and invest space with significance that flows from compositional importance. More: You can invest space with significance that also flows from symbolic meaning.

THE LAWN, 1996. Oil, gouache, and pencil (grease, charcoal, graphite) on canvas. 11 x 14 in. Private Collection, Sacramento, CA

MOVE & MEANING

IN MY WORK, I PLAY WHAT I TERM THE "VISUAL CHESS GAME OF MOVE & MEANING." A knight in chess moves as part of a game, but the knight also resonates with metaphorical meaning. We infer meaning from its form: a horse, on which the gallant knight rides. We infer meaning from the military and royal court associations evoked by the name of the chess piece—knight—and by the names of other chess pieces: bishop, rook (chariot), queen. And these associations get underscored by the symbolic nature of the game: a battle of two armies defending their king.

Inspired by the analogy of chess, I coined the term "Move & Meaning" to describe the double condition of every visual work: simultaneously compositional and metaphorical. Simultaneously an abstract aesthetic system and a symbolic image system. Simultaneously a system of chess-like moves and countermoves deployed in accord with abstract game theory and a system of chess-like symbols that triggers associational meaning. No matter how oblivious a painter or architect may be to this double condition, it can't be avoided. It defines every painting and building.

MOVE: Every painting is simultaneously a plan, section, and elevation, because every 2D picture is an abstract system of form-and-space relationships subject to multiple readings. Every 2D picture presents an aesthetic system: a compositional system—an architecture—for organizing the world.

MEANING: But every painting (and building) also conveys representational or metaphorical content, which emerges from the artist's calculated or inadvertent matrix of poetic allusions and explicit symbols that reference either the natural world or the world of ideas.

In my paintings, I concentrate on composition—Moves—because through painting, I seek to find the form and space of my architecture: its *Control*. I also infuse my paintings, some more overtly than others, with metaphors and allusions to the natural world and the world of ideas—Meaning—because through painting, I seek to find the narrative essence and philosophical foundation of my architecture: its *Soul*.

The next chapter of this book, "Practice," features a series of paintings that I call "ancient myths meet modern landscapes." Semiabstract "Figure|Field" pictures (I also call them "Field Paintings"), they present form-space chess moves and evoke the spirit of ancient insights into the patterns and conduct of life. Why ancient myths? Because they symbolize, for me, the timeless connection between the architecture of physical space and form and the architecture of the metaphysical structure of our lives.

So on one level, these paintings represent compositional forays into Cubist like simultaneity and ambiguity of plan, section, and elevation, expressions of the dialectic between 1) horizontal readings of the plane—abstracted vistas you could snapshot from an airplane: maps and site plans; and 2) vertical readings of the plane—abstracted vistas you could view looking toward the horizon: walls and windows.

But on another level, my paintings represent more than meets the eye. Not simply abstract spacecraft compositions, these paintings represent my attempts to create through the chess game of Move & Meaning the other side of the coin of Significant Space: space that also resonates with metaphorical and emotional meaning. My paintings reflect my quest to find the *Significant Form & Significant Space* of my architecture.

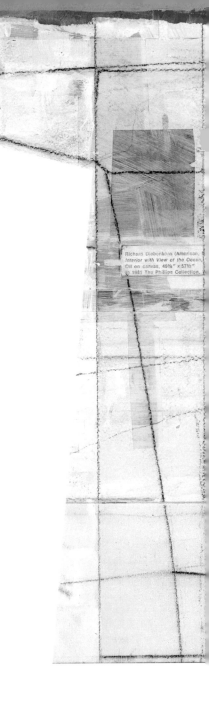

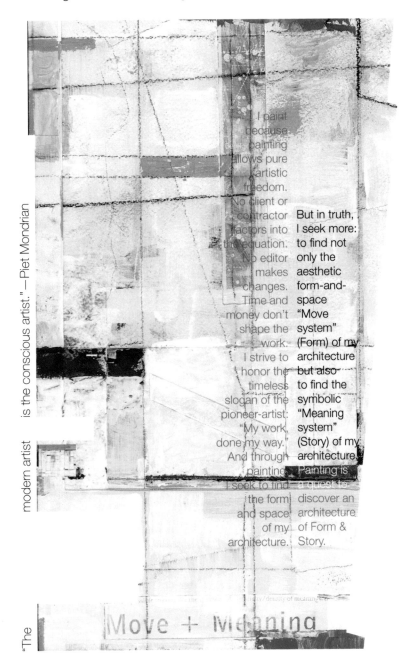

I paint because painting allows pure artistic freedom. No client or contractor factors into the equation. No editor makes changes. Time and money don't shape the work. I strive to honor the timeless slogan of the pioneer-artist: "My work, done my way." And through painting I seek to find the form and space of my architecture.

But in truth, I seek more: to find not only the aesthetic form-and-space "Move system" (Form) of my architecture but also to find the symbolic "Meaning system" (Story) of my architecture. Painting is a quest to discover an architecture of Form & Story.

"The modern artist is the conscious artist." — Piet Mondrian

Move + Meaning

Through painting,
I seek to find the Significant Form & Significant Space of my architecture—
the form-and-space Move & Meaning of my architecture.

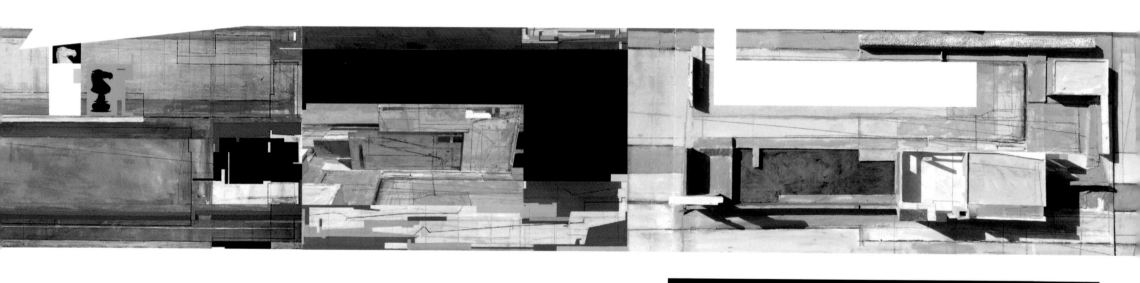

MOVE & MEANING

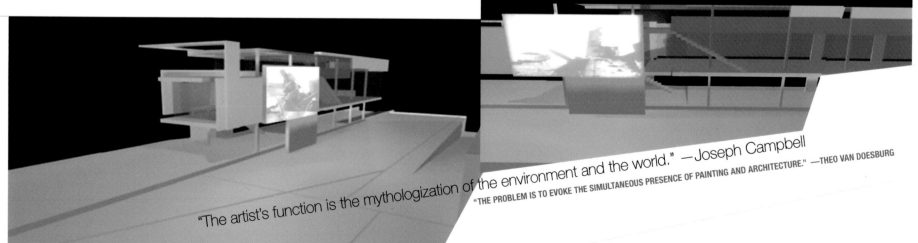

"The artist's function is the mythologization of the environment and the world." —Joseph Campbell

"THE PROBLEM IS TO EVOKE THE SIMULTANEOUS PRESENCE OF PAINTING AND ARCHITECTURE." —THEO VAN DOESBURG

THE IDEA OF NORTH

DANTE

WHERE AM I? The steel-beam Telescope (a shard of ancient suns) cuts through the Dante Monolith and sights the North Star.

WHERE AM I? The steel-beam Telescope (a shard of ancient suns) cuts through the Dante Monolith and sights the North Star.

IN A WORK OF ART, EVERYTHING MUST BE *FORMED*, BUT THE PURPOSE OF ART GOES BEYOND FORM:
"TO MAKE PERCEPTIBLE THE TEXTURE OF THE WORLD IN ALL ASPECTS." —BORIS MIKHAILOVICH EIKENBAUM

"The passage of the mythological hero may be overground, incidentally;

fundamentally it is inward—into depths where obscure resistances are overcome,

and long lost forgotten powers are revivified,

to be made available for the transfiguration of the world."

— Joseph Campbell, *The Hero with a Thousand Faces*

PRACTICE
ancient myths meet modern landscapes

Through painting,
I foreshadow an architecture of Form & Story.
ancient myths meet modern landscapes

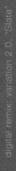

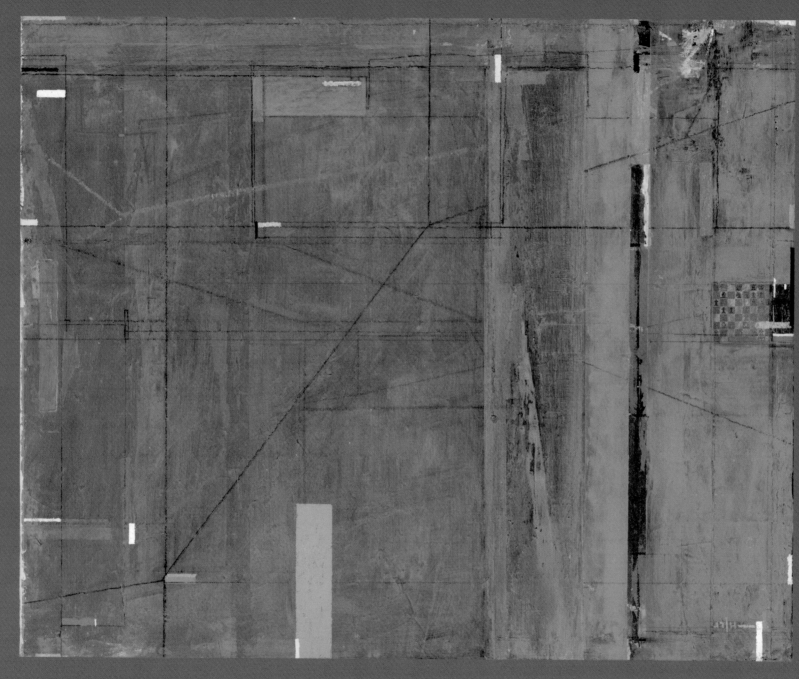

ITHACA

1996. oil and collage on canvas board in aluminum frame + pencil (grease, charcoal, graphite).16 x 20 in. | private collection, phoenix, az

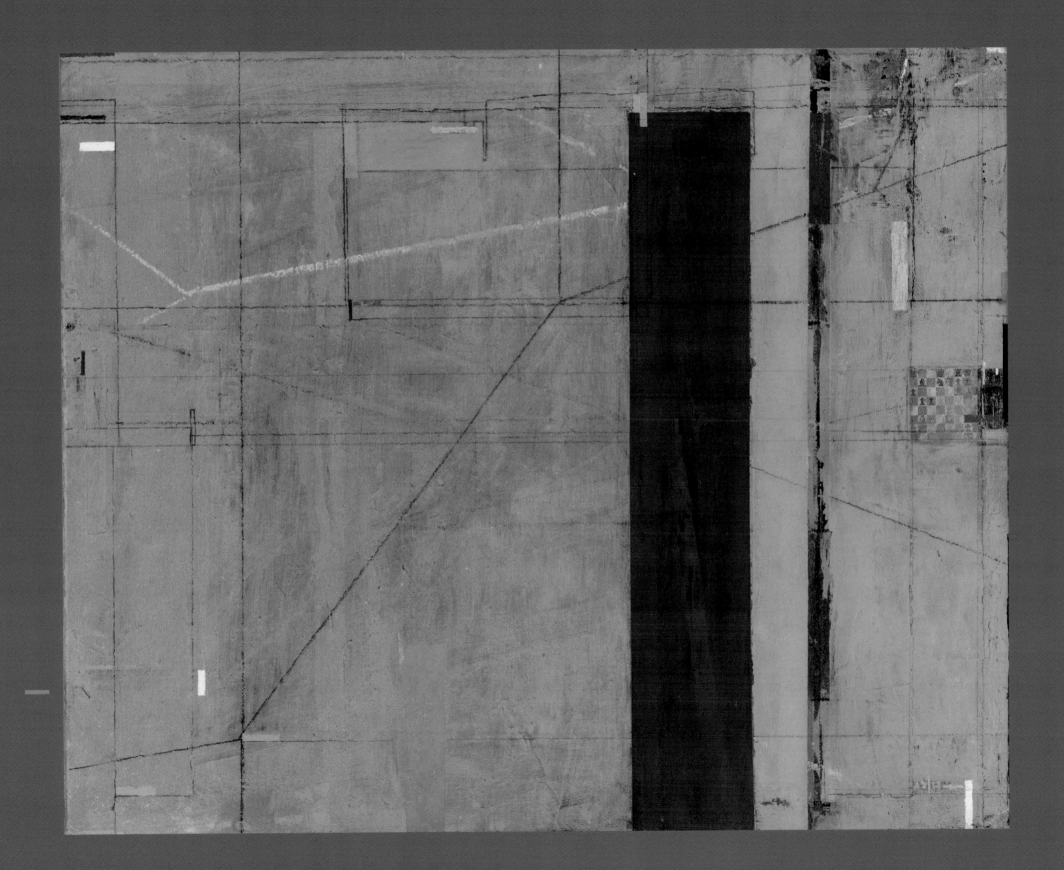

HOUSE OF THE HERO'S JOURNEY | (AKA MERCURY)

1996. oil on canvas in aluminum frame + pencil (grease, charcoal, graphite). 14 x 18 in.

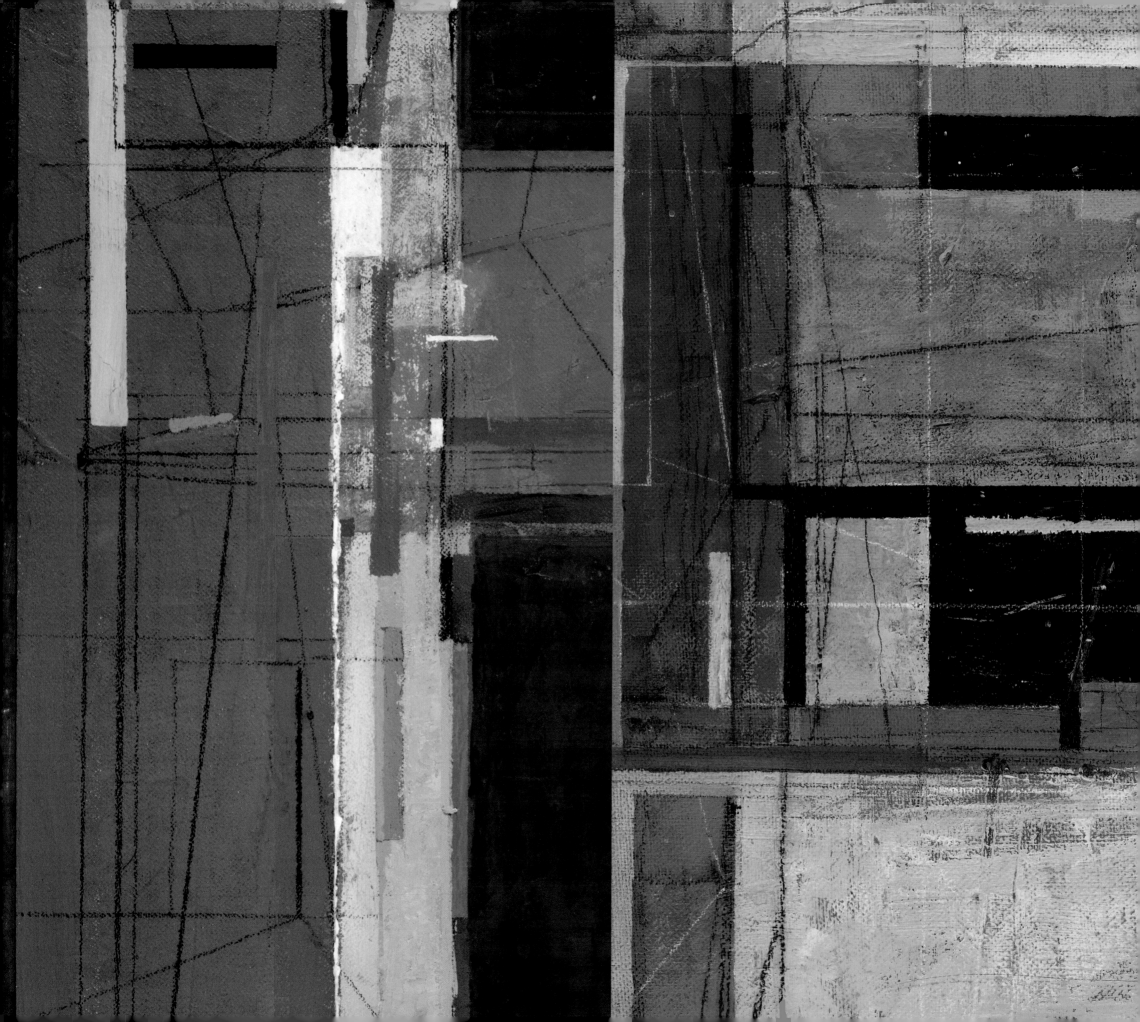

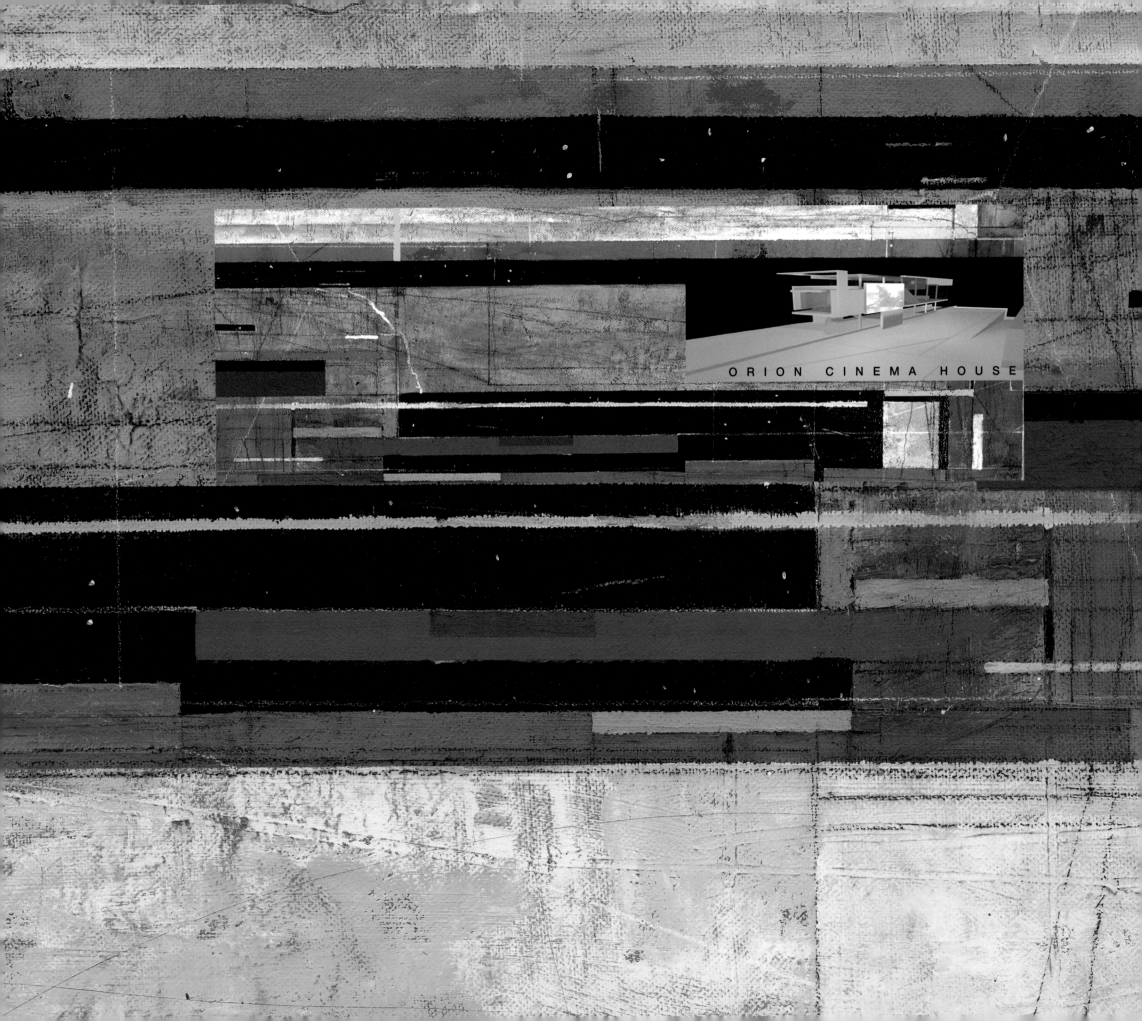

ORION CINEMA HOUSE

ORION CINEMA HOUSE | (AKA ORION)

1997. acrylic on canvas board in aluminum frame + pencil (grease, charcoal, graphite). 16 x 20 in. | private collection, new york, ny

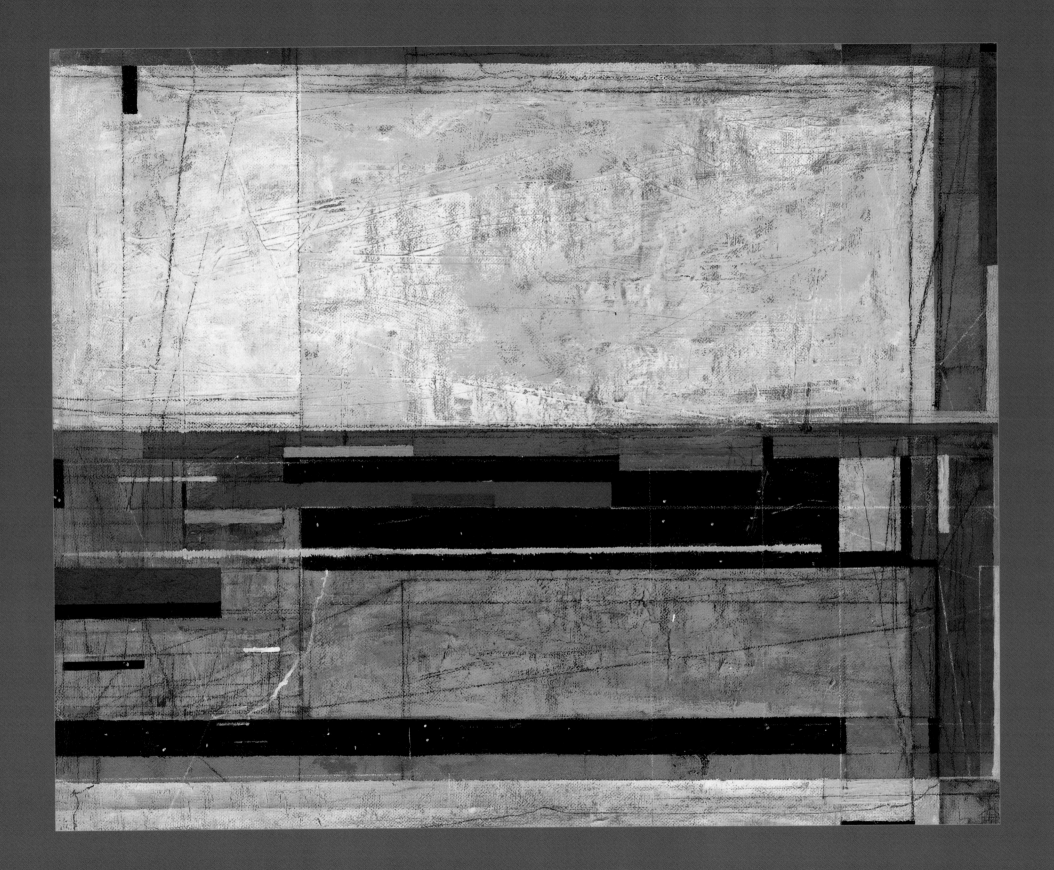

HERO'S JOURNEY

1996. acrylic and collage on wood + pencil (grease, charcoal, graphite). 14 x 18 in.

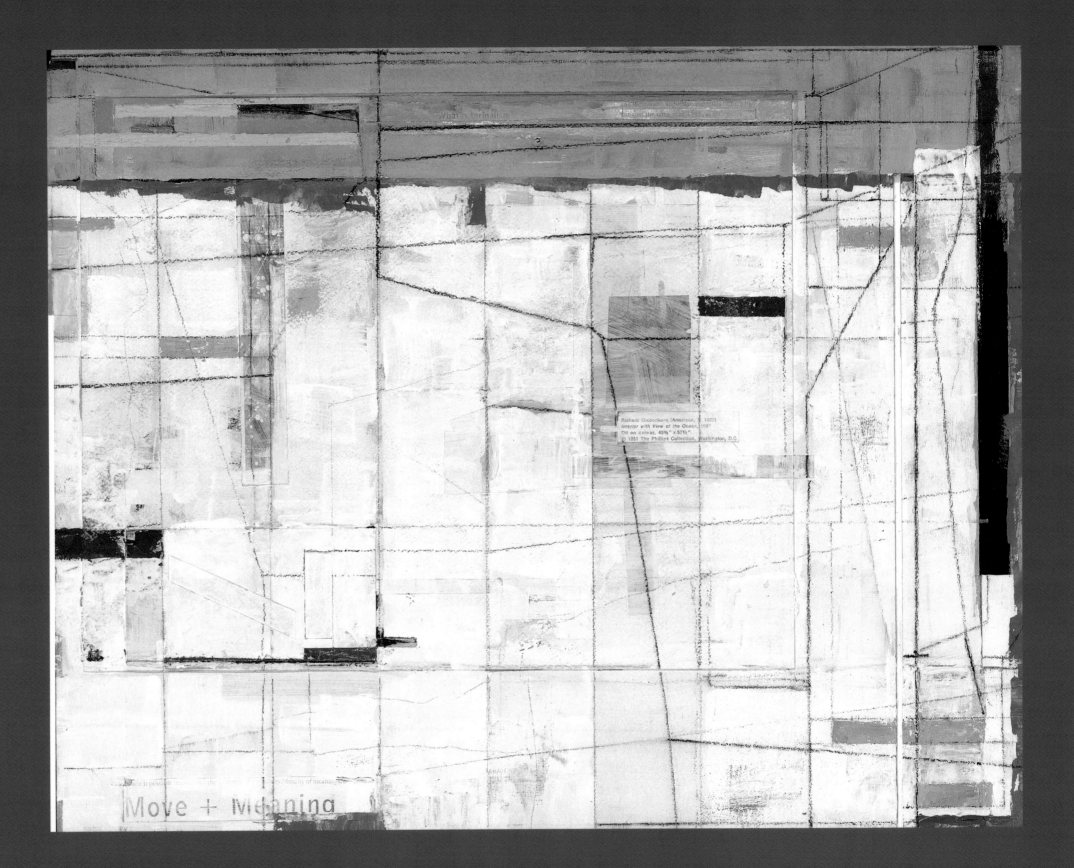

What is formalism?

Richard Diebenkorn, (American, b. 1922)
Interior with View of the Ocean, 1957
Oil on canvas, 49¼" x 57½"
© 1981 The Phillips Collection, Washington, D.C.

Move + Meaning

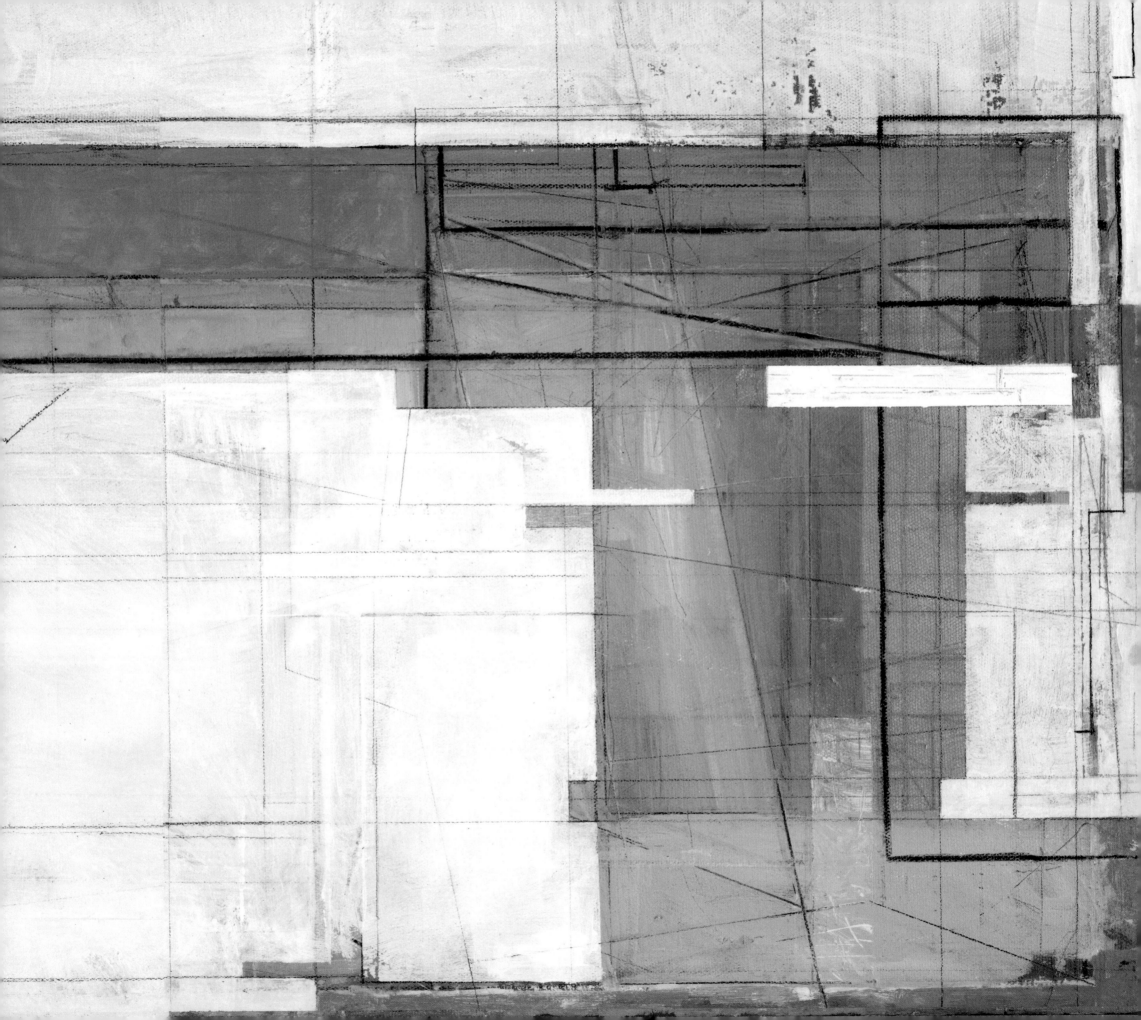

56 HENRYTRUCKS

DAEDALUS'S LABYRINTH

1997. oil on canvas in aluminum frame + pencil (grease, charcoal, graphite). 18 x 24 in.

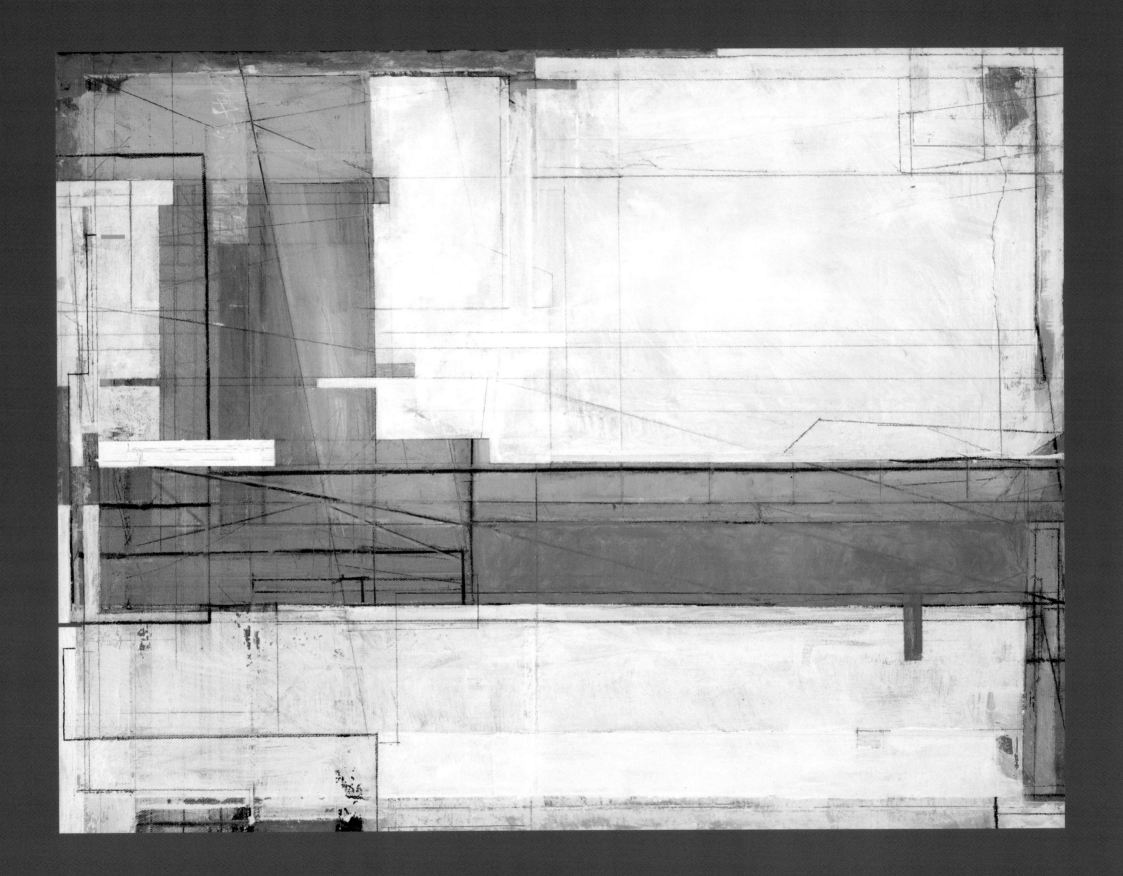

ULYSSES

1997. oil on canvas in aluminum frame + pencil (grease, charcoal, graphite). 24.625 x 38.5 in. | private collection, sacramento, ca

DAEDALUS | (AKA AENEAS : SELF-PORTRAIT : THE KNIGHT)

1996. oil on canvas in aluminum frame + pencil (grease, charcoal, graphite). 24.625 x 38.5 in. | private collection, boston, ma

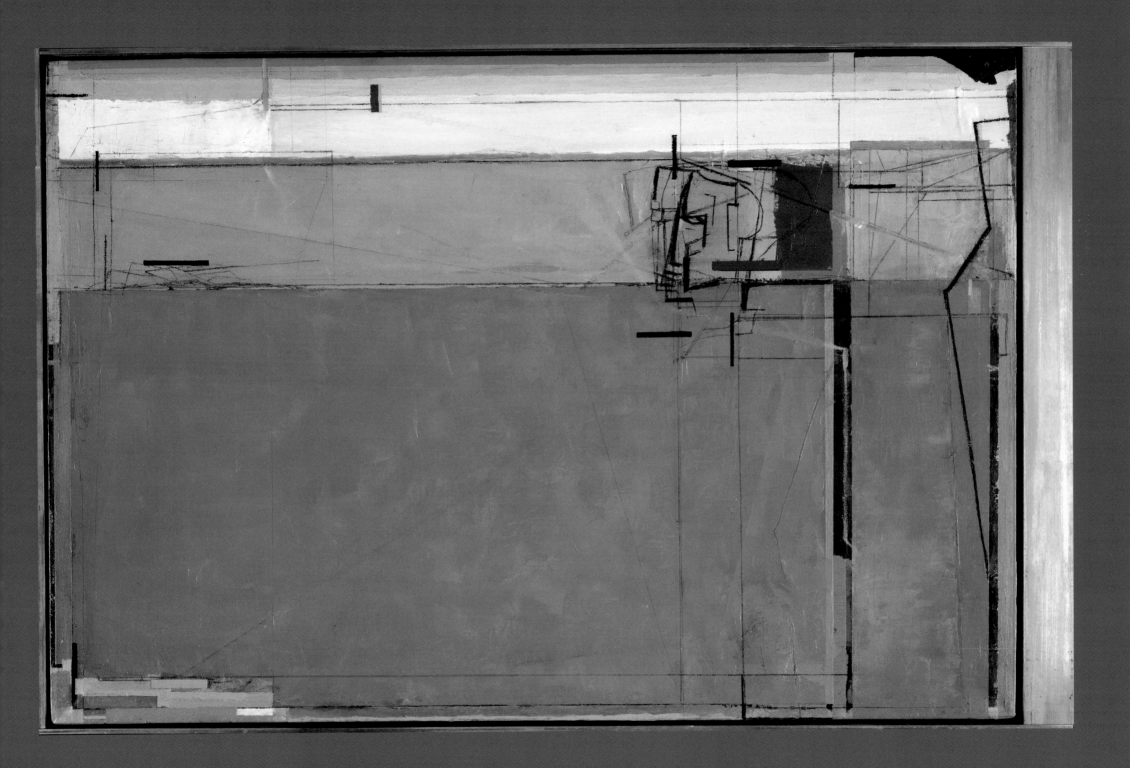

DAEDALUS | digital remix 1.0

DAEDALUS | digital remix 2.0

68 HENRYTRUCKS

TEMPLE OF THE ANCIENT KNIGHT | (AKA SHIP)

1997. acrylic on canvas + pencil (grease, charcoal, graphite). 30 x 40 in.

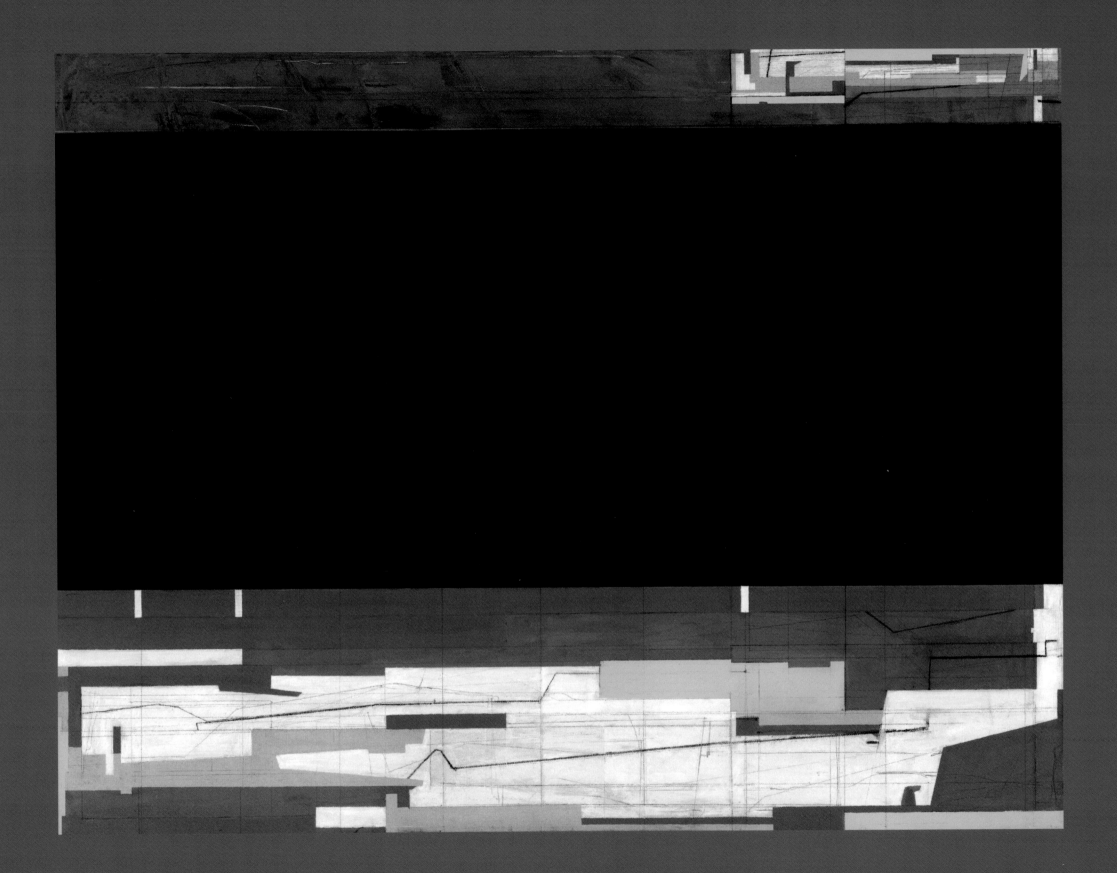

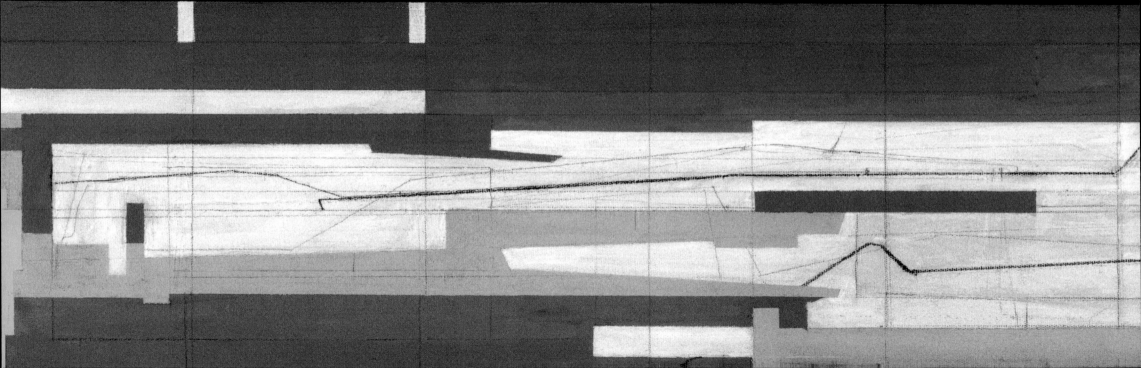

CRETE

1998. oil on canvas + pencil (graphite). 36 x 60 in.

TROY

1998. oil and collage on canvas + pencil (grease, charcoal, graphite). 36 x 60 in.

TROY | digital remix [1.0]

SELF-PORTRAIT, 2000 | BALTIMORE

HENRYTRUCKS

SELF-PORTRAIT, 2012 | SACRAMENTO

ODYSSEY

ODYSSEY | original

2009 – unfinished. oil on canvas + pencil (grease, charcoal, graphite). 48 x 72 in.

paint-over leading to status on pp. 82–83

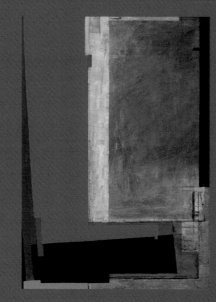

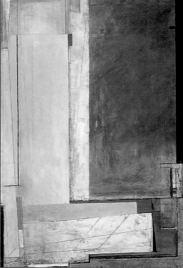

T R O J A N   H O R S E

1997–2002. oil on canvas + pencil (grease, charcoal, graphite). 30 x 40 in.

LABYRINTH | (AKA DAEDALUS)

1996. acrylic on canvas in wood frame + pencil (grease, charcoal, graphite). 24 x 36 in. | private collection, williamstown, ma

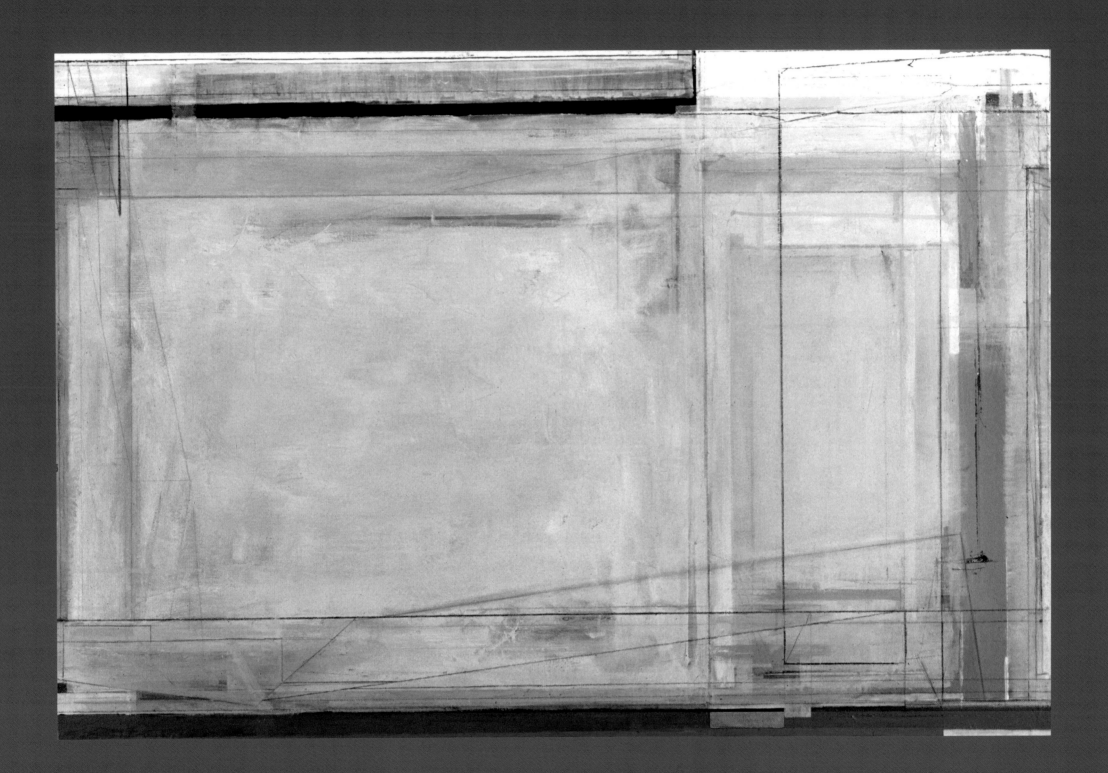

LABYRINTH ii : TOWER, MAZE, AND LAWN

1998. oil on canvas in aluminum frame + pencil (grease, charcoal, graphite). 30 x 40 in. | private collection, boston, ma

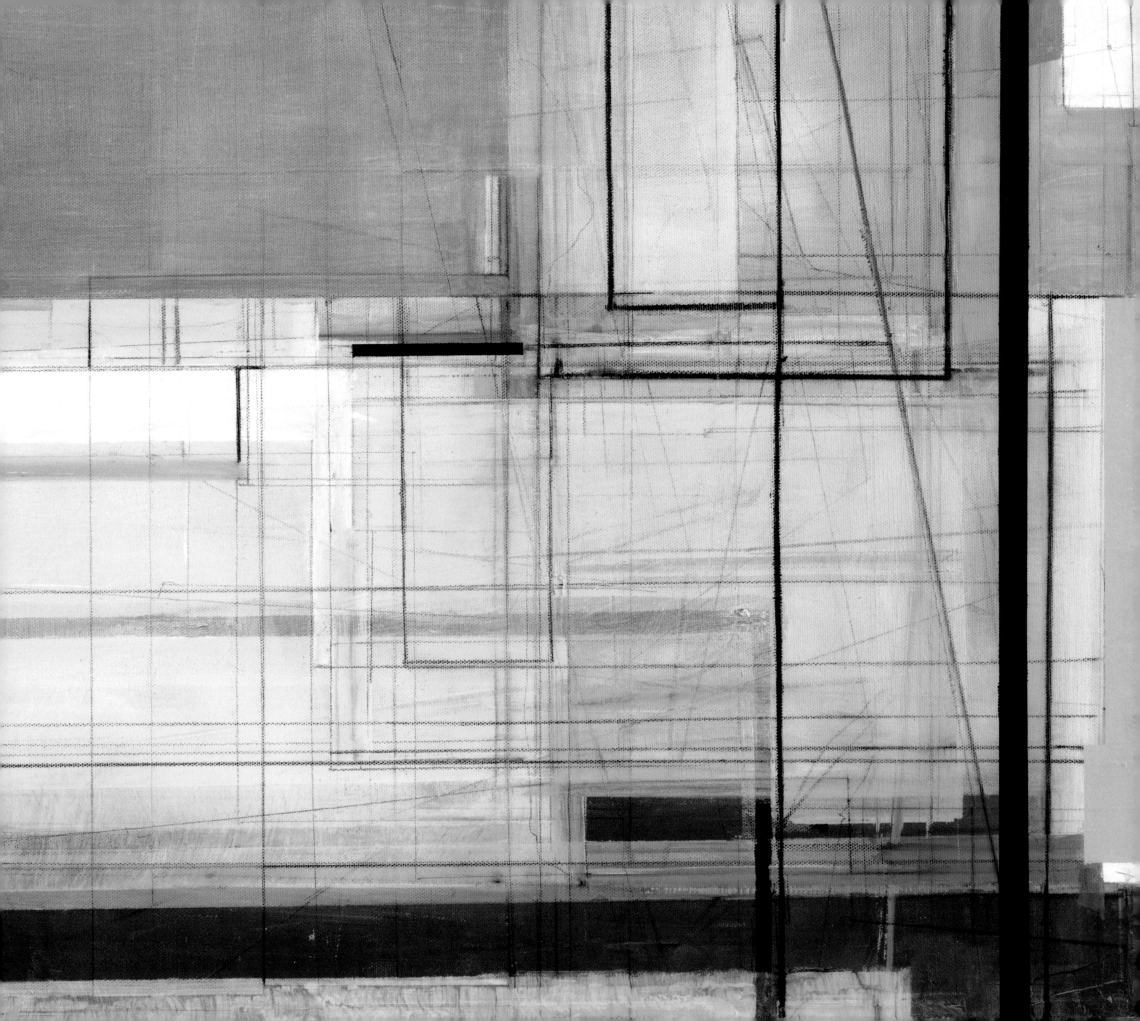

LABYRINTH ii : TOWER, MAZE, AND LAWN │ digital remix 2.0

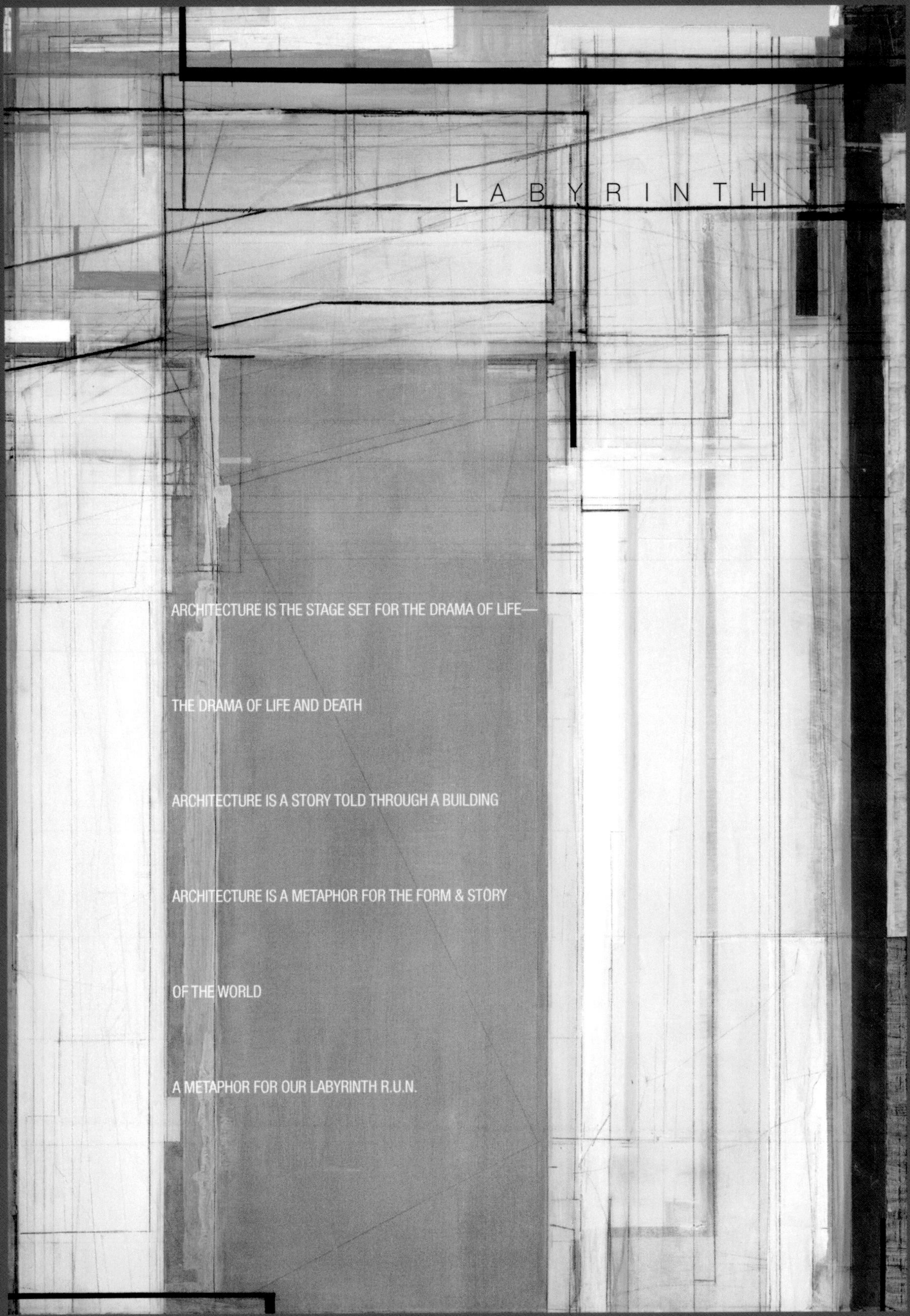

LABYRINTH

ARCHITECTURE IS THE STAGE SET FOR THE DRAMA OF LIFE—

THE DRAMA OF LIFE AND DEATH

ARCHITECTURE IS A STORY TOLD THROUGH A BUILDING

ARCHITECTURE IS A METAPHOR FOR THE FORM & STORY

OF THE WORLD

A METAPHOR FOR OUR LABYRINTH R.U.N.

MARINER

2001. oil on canvas + pencil (grease, charcoal, graphite). 30 x 40 in. | private collection, santa barbara, ca

OCEAN VOYAGE

1996. acrylic and collage on canvas + pencil (grease, charcoal, graphite). 14 x 18 in.

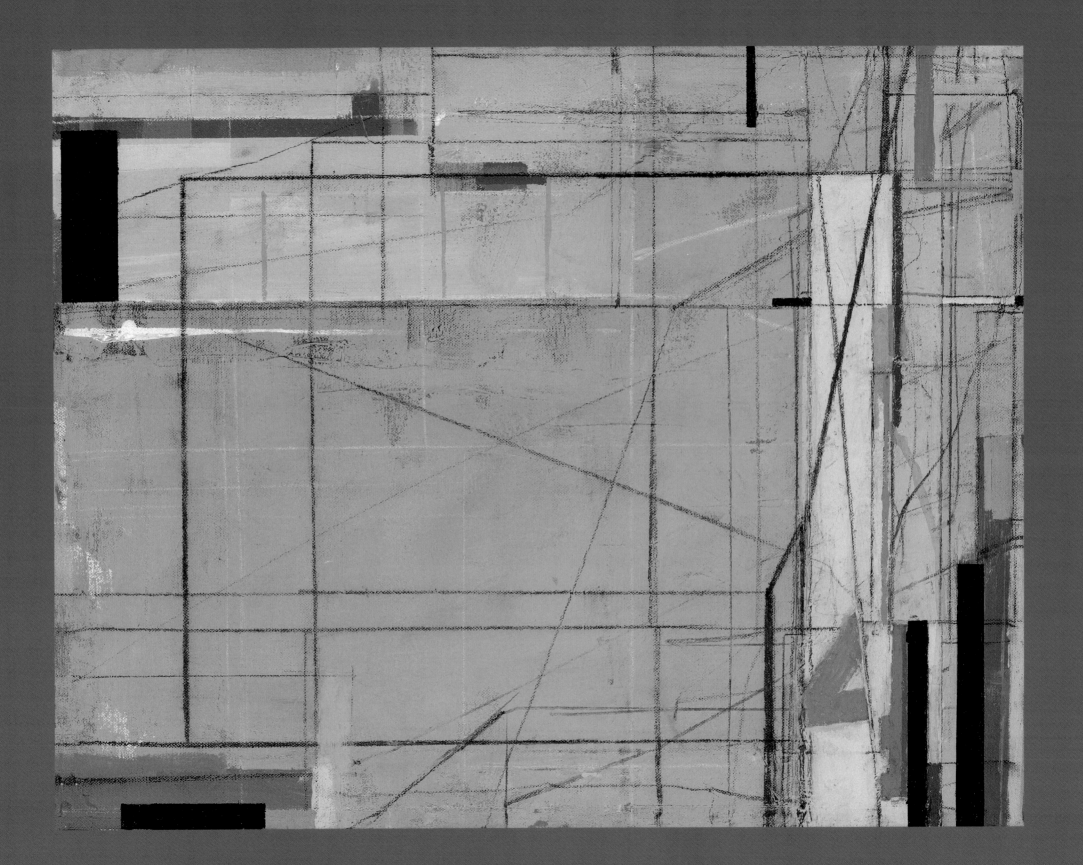

PENELOPE'S WINDOW

1997. oil on canvas in wood frame + pencil (grease, charcoal, graphite). 24 x 36 in.

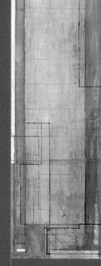

early version, before I painted over it

DAEDALUS HQ | (AKA HOME : THE CHAMBER OF THE SILVER KNIGHT)

1999–2002. acrylic on canvas + pencil (grease, charcoal, graphite). 24 x 36 in. | private collection, new york, ny

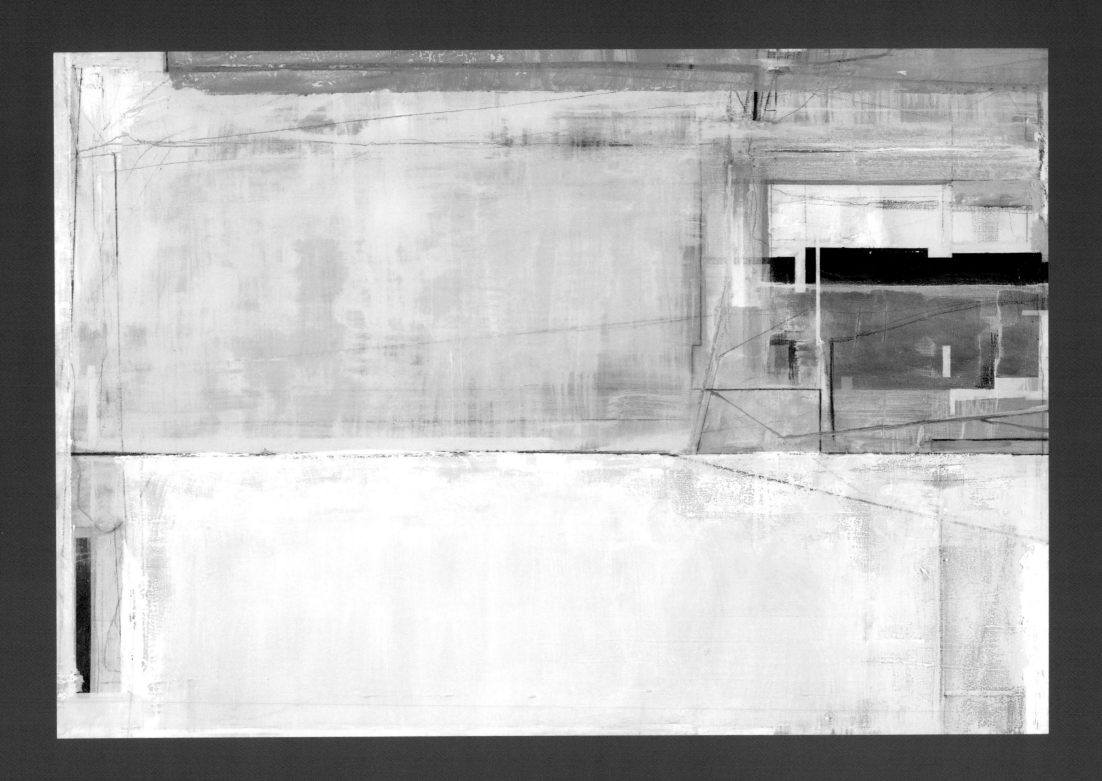

DEPARTURE | TRANSFORMATION | RETURN

LABYRINTH R.U.N.

"A hero ventures forth from the world of common day into a region
—Joseph Campbell, *The Hero with a Thousand Faces* (1949)

THE HERO'S JOURNEY HOUSE
JEF7REY HILDNER | ARCHITECT

DAEDALUS HQ

ARCHITECTURE IS A HERO'S JOURNEY | THROUGH THE LABYRINTH: TOWER, MAZE, AND LAWN

HOME

THE CHAMBER OF THE SILVER KNIGHT

of supernatural wonder: fabulous forces are there encountered and a decisive victory is won: the hero comes back from this mysterious adventure with the power to bestow boons on his fellow man."

HOUSE OF THE WHITE KNIGHT | (AKA ACROPOLIS)

1998. acrylic on canvas + pencil (grease, charcoal, graphite). 36 x 60 in. | private collection, boston, ma

STONEHENGE VILLA | (AKA TELESCOPE : LIGHTHOUSE)

1997. acrylic on canvas + pencil (grease, charcoal, graphite). 30 x 40 in.

STONEHENGE VILLA | digital remix ¹·⁰

STONEHENGE VILLA | digital remix 2.0

ARCHITECTURE IS A CHESS GAME OF FORM & STORY
PLAYED ON THE AESTHETIC & SYMBOLIC RECTANGLE OF ART

JUST. LIKE. A. MOVIE.

The steel-beam Telescope juts into the night sky toward the North Star . . .

(D)ANTE | TELESCOPE HOUSE 1991–1996. PHOTOGRAPH © YUKIO FUTAGAWA | GA PHOTOGRAPHERS. *GA HOUSES #51*, 1997

ARCHITECTURE IS THE STAGE SET FOR THE DRAMA OF LIFE—
THE DRAMA OF LIFE AND DEATH

ARCHITECTURE IS A STORY TOLD THROUGH A BUILDING

THE WHITE KNIGHT OF FORM + THE BLACK KNIGHT OF STORY =
THE SILVER KNIGHT OF FORM & STORY | MY AVATAR

| THE ARMIES OF FORM & STORY FIGHT THE WAR OF ART | THEY FIGHT FOR OUR MIND AND SOUL AND HEART

ART IS A VISION QUEST

STONEHENGE VILLA | digital remix 3.0
HENRYTRUCKS

ART IS A CHESS GAME OF FORM & STORY WAGED ON THE BATTLEFIELD OF THE AESTHETIC & SYMBOLIC RECTANGLE
WALL, CANVAS, PAGE, AND SCREEN

THE ARMIES OF FORM & STORY FIGHT THE WAR OF ART
THEY FIGHT FOR OUR MIND AND SOUL AND HEART

GARDEN OF DAEDALUS'S RETURN | (AKA HARBOR)

1998. oil on canvas + pencil (grease, charcoal, graphite). 30 x 40 in.

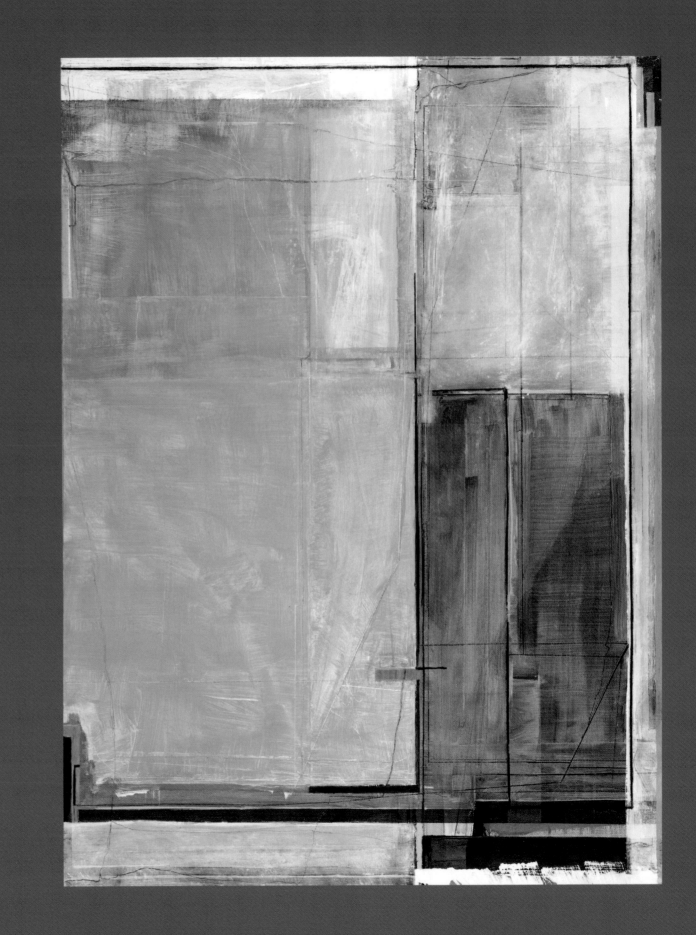

GARDEN OF DAEDALUS'S RETURN | digital remix[1.0]

BUT WHATEVER DISASTERS BEFALL, DO NOT FLINCH.

GO ALL THE BOLDER TO FACE THEM, FOLLOW YOUR FATE

TO THE LIMIT. A ROAD WILL OPEN TO SAFETY

FROM THE LAST PLACE YOU WOULD EXPECT . . .

—VIRGIL | THE AENEID

ICARUS

2009. oil on canvas. 48 x 72 in.

FLIGHT MASTER

Daedalus murdered his sister's son Talus.
Envy of the nephew's talents spurred
Daedalus's monstrous crime.
King of Athens, the city his grandfather
Erechtheus built,
Fallen Daedalus fled to Crete for solace.

Who are you, single-hearted Daedalus?
Craftsman for Queen Pasiphaë's desire,
Designer for King Minos's wrath,
Rescuer of their daughter Ariadne's heart:
So her Theseus could slay the Minotaur,
You unspooled the secret of your Labyrinth.

How shall I know you, King Daedalus?
Creator of wings, spinner of yarns, architect,
Thought-hero of thunderous imagination,
Brave truth-seeker of art, beyond time.
Or simply as you know yourself?
Sad father who lost dear Icarus to the sun.

"[Daedalus] is the hero of the way of thought—singlehearted, courageous, and full of faith that the truth, as he finds it, shall make us free.

And so now we may turn to him, as did Ariadne. The flax for the linen of his thread he has gathered from the fields of the human imagination."

—Joseph Campbell, *The Hero with a Thousand Faces*

FLIGHT MASTER

2010. oil on canvas + pencil (grease, charcoal, graphite). 62 x 93 in.

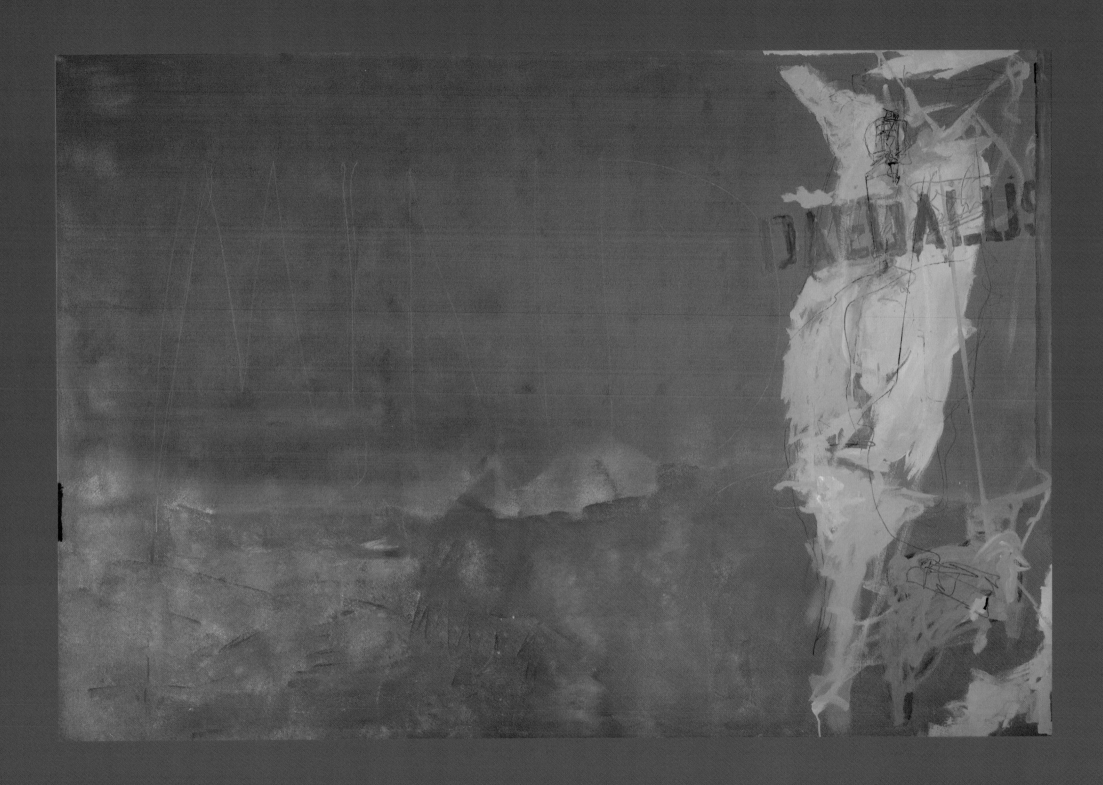

"Great musicians are like great fighters.

They have a higher sense of theory going on in their heads."

—Miles Davis

CODA

**?+__###@|~~————————

Composition is a game, and a game has rules.

ARCHITECTURE AS PAINTING. DANTE | TELESCOPE HOUSE (AKA THE ZLOWE HOUSE). SILVER SPRING, MD | 1991–1996. INTERIOR WORLD SHAPED BY THE DANTE MONOLITH SHADOW ZONE, FEATURING THE "NORTH STAR TELESCOPE RUG," "TELESCOPE WALL LAMP," AND "1:4:9 OBSERVATORY CHESS MURAL."

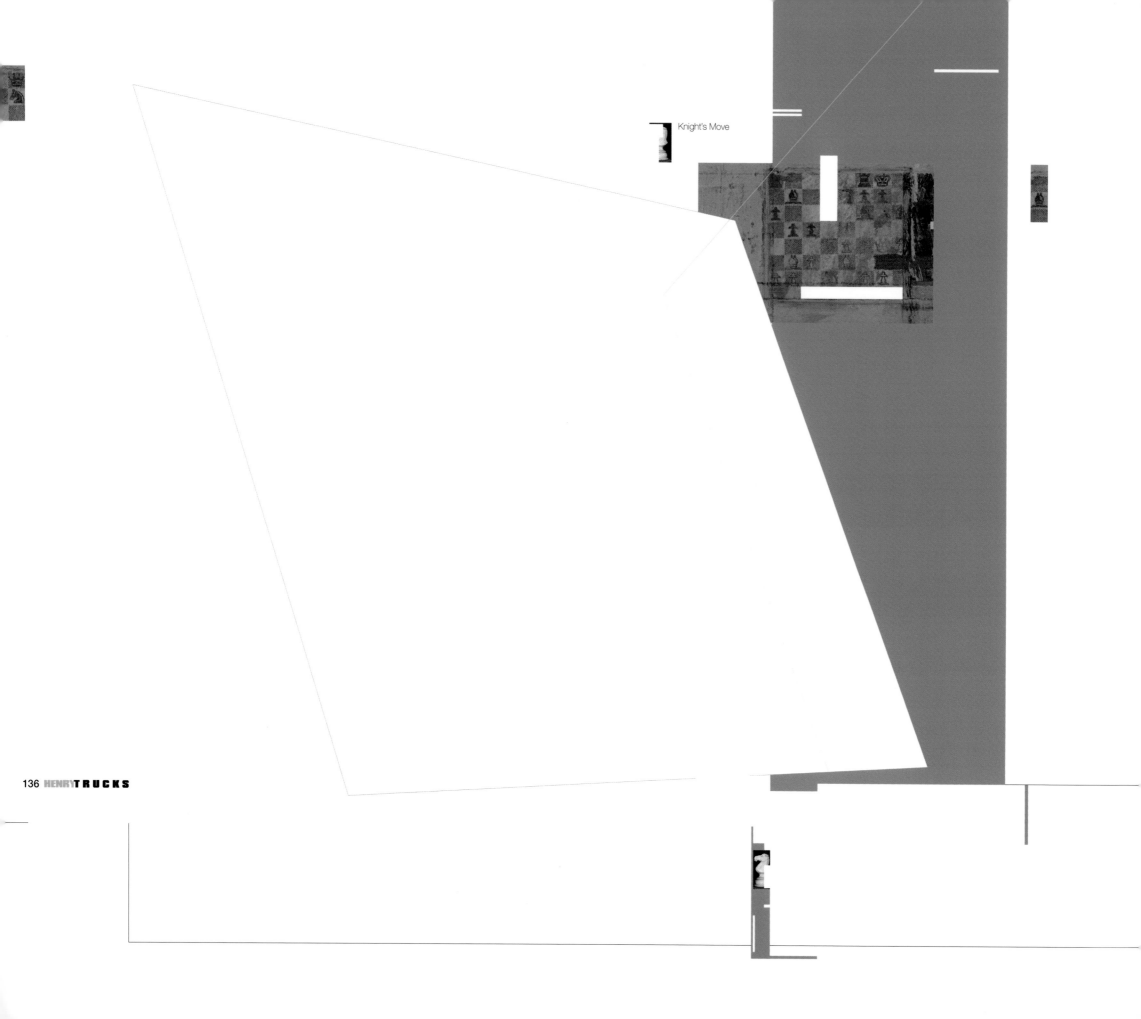

Knight's Move

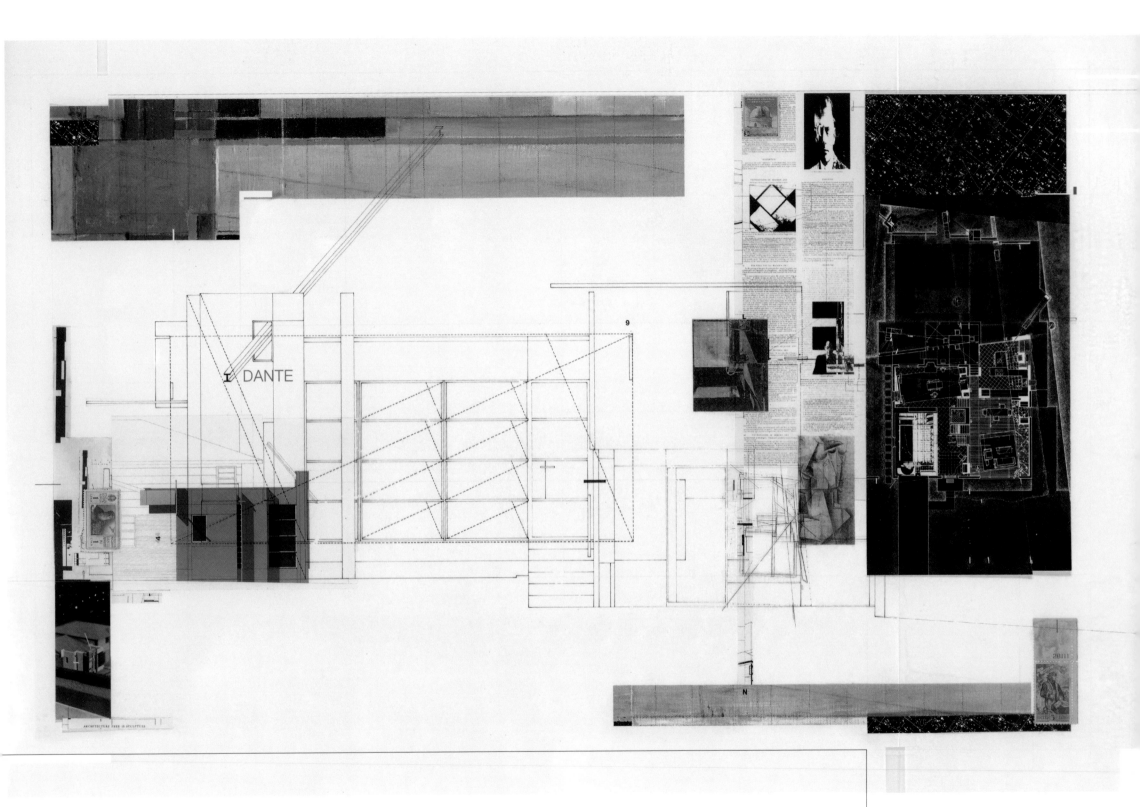

DANTE | TELESCOPE HOUSE

"If you're going to paint, you'd better find out why you're doing it, and you should do something that you know about, that you're infatuated with." —Wayne Thiebaud

I WORK ON THE ARCHITECTURE OF THE RECTANGLE: THE AESTHETIC & SYMBOLIC RECTANGLE

MOVE & MEANING

PRETTY AND GRITTY
CONTROL AND SOUL

DANTE | TELESCOPE HOUSE 1:4:9 OBSERVATORY CHESS MURAL

DAEDALUS

KHQ

ionshi

"INSPIRATION DOES EXIST, BUT IT MUST FIND US WORKING." | PICASSO

DUET | 1994–1997. 54 x 54 in.
PART 1 | RICHARD ROSA, 1994
House paint on canvas + graphite, chalk, oil pastel, and satin marine varnish
PART 2 | JEF7REY HILDNER, 1997
Oil on pre-painted canvas + graphite, grease pencil, pasted paper | sheet lead & nails

KNIGHT   HEADQUARTERS | HOUSE   OF   THE   SILVER   KNIGHT

FIGURAL VOID

THURSDAY, DAY,

"[DAEDALUS] IS THE HERO OF THE WAY OF THOUGHT—

SINGLEHEARTED, COURAGEOUS, AND FULL OF

FAITH THAT THE TRUTH, AS HE FINDS IT, SHALL

HERO'S JOURNEY

MAKE US FREE. AND SO NOW WE MAY TURN TO HIM,

AS DID ARIADNE. THE FLAX FOR THE LINEN OF HIS

THREAD HE HAS GATHERED FROM THE FIELDS OF

THE HUMAN IMAGINATION."

— JOSEPH CAMPBELL, *THE HERO WITH A THOUSAND FACES*

Photography by Mimi L. —Donald
Apple Hill Country Collection
0125

A WALL IS A CANVAS. AND A CANVAS IS A WALL.

I paint because painting allows pure artistic freedom. No client or contractor factors into the equation. No editor makes changes. Time and money don't shape the work. I strive to honor the timeless slogan of the pioneer-artist: "My work, done my way." And through painting, I seek to find the form and space of my architecture.

But in truth, I seek more: to find not only the aesthetic form-and-space "Move-system" (Form) of my architecture but also to find the symbolic "Meaning-system" (Story) of my architecture. Painting is a quest to discover an architecture of Form & Story.

PRINCETON STUDIO | *Gray Square, Brook, and Smoke*

HERALD-CALL HAIKU
ARCHITECT THE TALE OF HERO DAEDALUS'S TREK — TIMELESS VISION QUEST.

17

THE DAEDALUS PROJECT: THE HERO'S JOURNEY HOUSE

A L U S

9

"We bring to our projects the architecture of ourselves." — Mikhail Bakhtin

GARDE

HOUSE OF THE METAPHYSICAL WARRIOR
HOUSE OF THE SILVER KNIGHT

KnightHeadQuarters

HILDNER |JEF7REY

archive.org/details/Jef7reyHildnerArchitect-QFB

Some images shown in this volume represent digital remixes of original paintings. Remixes range from adjustments of painting elements and color spectrum to changes of the ratio of the canvas size.

THE ARCHITECT PAINTER PRESS offers Fine Art Giclée Prints on canvas or paper either of an original painting match or of a custom digital remix.

contact: 7@thearchitectpainterpress.com

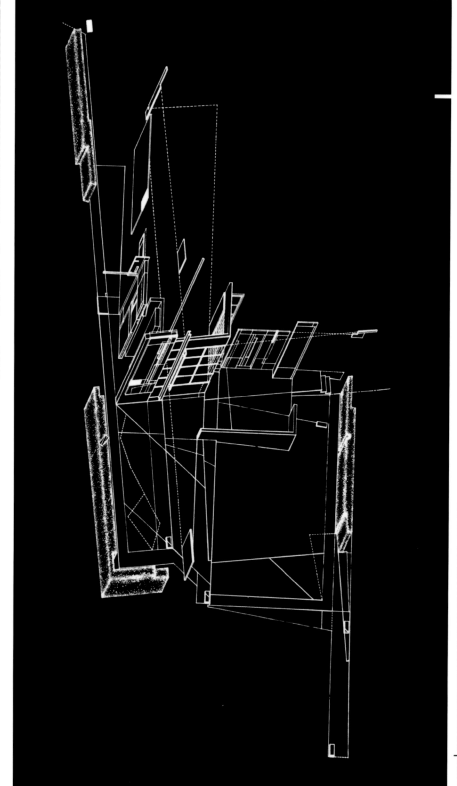

DANTE | **TELESCOPE HOUSE** (AKA ZLOWE HOUSE), JEF7REY HILDNER ARCHITECT. AXONOMETRIC OF SPACE-DEFINING ELEMENTS | 1991–1996

YOUR PATH TO SAFETY WILL OPEN FIRST
FROM WHERE YOU LEAST EXPECT IT
—VIRGIL | THE AENEID

SUBSTRATE: ULYSSES REMIX | Ulysses, 1997 | oil on canvas in aluminum frame + pencil (grease, charcoal, graphite, 24.625 x 38.5 in | private collection: sacramento.ca

ART IS A VISION QUEST : A SEARCH FOR A SIGNIFICANT SPACE-MAKING AESTHETIC SYSTEM & A SIGNIFICANT SYMBOLIC IMAGE SYSTEM — AN ARCHITECTURE OF FORM & STORY

empty space | full space

"Space is shaped. Space is full of curves and dents and wonderful shapes."
— Albert Einstein, Peter Moffat's screenplay *Einstein and Eddington*

P   A   I   N   T   E   R

20 WORKS

148 HENRY**TRUCKS**

CONTROLANDSOUL

2237 GALLERY. ROSEVILLE CALIFORNIA. FEBRUARY 11 - MAY 9   2013.

"Precisely because it is the familiar way, it is not the artistic way." —Victor Shklovsky, "Art as Device" | 1917

HENRY**TRUCKS**

THE PROBLEM IS TO EVOKE THE SIMULTANEOUS PRESENCE OF PAINTING AND ARCHITECTURE. —Theo van Doesburg | 1917

The steel-beam telescope sights the North Star...

ITHACA COLLAGE. Dante | Telescope House, digital collage. 40 x 40 in.
International "Art in Architecture" Exhibition, The Center for Contemporary Art, Bedminster, New Jersey, 2010

the visual = the visible + the invisible

:art

ALSO BY JEF7REY HILDNER

VISUAL EF9ECTS
ARCHITECTURE AND THE CHESS GAME OF
FORM & STORY

ARCHITECTURE IS A CHESS GAME OF FORM & STORY WAGED ON THE BATTLEFIELD
OF A BUILDING AND ITS SITE

The White Army of **FORM** cries,
"ARCHITECTURE IS THE STAGE SET FOR THE DRAMA OF LIFE."

The Black Army of **STORY** cries,
"ARCHITECTURE IS A STORY TOLD THROUGH A BUILDING."

IN VISUAL EF9ECTS,
ARCHITECT JEF7REY HILDNER
BUILDS ON SIGNATURE THEMES AND
CONCEPTS THAT HE LAID OUT IN HIS
BOOK *DAEDALUS 9*, TURNING AGAIN
TO THE CINEMATIC METAPHOR OF
CHESS TO BRING HIS THEORY OF
ARCHITECTURE TO LIFE. AN AWARD-
WINNING SCREENWRITER AS WELL
AS AN AWARD-WINNING ARCHITECT,
HILDNER TRANSPOSES INSIGHTS FROM
THE ARENA OF STORY ARCHITECTURE
TO HIS PARALLEL ARENA OF BUILDING
ARCHITECTURE. *VISUAL EF9ECTS*
REFLECTS HIS QUEST TO DESIGN
BUILDINGS THAT PRESENT A CREATIVE
DEMONSTRATION OF THE CHESS GAME
OF ART, WHERE THE WHITE ARMY OF
FORM (AESTHETICS) AND THE BLACK
ARMY OF STORY (SYMBOLICS) BATTLE
FOR OUR MIND AND SOUL AND HEART—
FORM & STORY FIGHT TO CREATE A
HEART-POUNDING WORK OF ART.

SELF-PORTRAIT, 2012 | SACHAMENTO

SILVER KNIGHT ARCHITECTURE

Knight HeadQuarters

THE WHITE KNIGHT OF AESTHETICS: F O R M
+
THE BLACK KNIGHT OF SYMBOLICS: STORY
=
THE SILVER KNIGHT OF ART

MY AVATAR

7

LIFE-SIZE CHESS GAME ON PALACE SQUARE,
ST. PETERSBURG, 1924

KHQ

7

"GREAT ART IS THE OUTWARD EXPRESSION OF AN INNER LIFE OF THE ARTIST,"
AND THIS INNER LIFE WILL RESULT IN HIS PERSONAL VISION OF THE WORLD."
—EDWARD HOPPER

THE SILVER KNIGHT OF FORM & STORY

7

150 HENRY **TRUCKS**

archive.org/details/VisualEf9ects

ART IS A CHESS GAME OF FORM & STORY WAGED ON THE BATTLEFIELD OF OUR MIND AND SOUL AND HEART
THE ARMIES OF FORM & STORY FIGHT THE WAR OF ART | THEY FIGHT FOR OUR MIND AND SOUL AND HEART

to learn more about the author, go to:
archive.org/details/Jef7reyHIldnerArchitect-QFB